Present at the Creation

Secretary of State George C. Marshall receiving the honorary Doctor of Laws degree from Dr. Reginald Fitz, the University Marshal, at Harvard University commencement, 5 June 1947.

PRESENT AT THE CREATION

The Fortieth Anniversary
of the Marshall Plan

CONFERENCE SERIES ORGANIZED BY THE
LUXEMBOURG-HARVARD ASSOCIATION
WITH HARVARD UNIVERSITY

EDITED BY

ARMAND CLESSE

AND

ARCHIE C. EPPS

1817

Harper & Row, Publishers, New York

BALLINGER DIVISION

Grand Rapids, Philadelphia, St. Louis, San Francisco
London, Singapore, Sydney, Tokyo, Toronto

The title of this book is that of Dean Acheson's memoir, Present at the Creation *(New York: W. W. Norton, 1969). It is used here to convey the notion that many of the contributors to this volume helped design and implement the Marshall Plan in its early stages.*

Frontispiece reprinted courtesy of the Harvard University Archives.

Secretary of State George C. Marshall's address at Harvard commencement, 5 June 1947, is reprinted with the permission of the President and Fellows of Harvard College.

International Standard Book Number: 0–88730–405–2

Library of Congress Catalog Card Number: 89–26688

Printed in the United States of America

Library of Congress Cataloging-in-Publication Data

Present at the creation: the fortieth anniversary of the Marshall Plan: conference series organized by the Luxembourg-Harvard Association with Harvard University / edited by Armand Clesse and Archie C. Epps.
    p. cm.
  ISBN 0–88730–405–2
  1. Marshall Plan—Congresses. 2. Economic assistance, American—Europe—Congresses. 3. Europe—Economic conditions—1945—Congresses. I. Clesse, Armand. II. Epps, Archie C. III. Luxembourg-Harvard Association. IV. Harvard University.
HC240.P68 1990
338.9'17304—dc20   89–26688
                                                                     CIP

89 90 91 92 HC 9 8 7 6 5 4 3 2 1

This book is dedicated with gratitude to Jacques Santer,
Prime Minister of Luxembourg.

Contents

vii

Preface

In December 1987, a conference was convened in Luxembourg on the fortieth anniversary of the announcement of the Marshall Plan at the Harvard University commencement in June 1947. The conference was convened by the Luxembourg-Harvard Association with Dr. Armand Clesse as president. The prime minister of Luxembourg, Jacques Santer, had granted the mandate to discuss the origins of the plan and how it was carried out. Attending the conference were civil servants who had assisted General George Marshall and were present when the plan was created. Conference participants were also selected from among the Europeans and Americans who had helped put the plan into action. The keynote speaker was Ambassador Arthur Hartman, who had heard Marshall's historic speech in Harvard Yard as a graduating senior.

The speech expressed in a few words a farsighted and generous policy that spoke well for the United States and would help to restore to the Europeans the courage and the confidence to rebuild their shattered economies and find a new place for themselves in the life of the world. General Marshall said:

Our policy is directed not against any country or doctrine but against hunger, poverty, desperation, and chaos. Its purpose should be the revival of a working economy in the world, so as to permit the emergence of political and social conditions in which free institutions can exist. Such assistance, I am convinced, must not be on a piecemeal basis as various crises develop. Any assistance that this government may render in the future should provide a cure rather than a mere palliative. Any government that is willing to assist in the task of recovery will find full cooperation, I am sure, on the part of the United States government. Any government which maneuvers to block the recovery of other countries cannot expect help from us. Furthermore, governments, political parties, or groups which seek to perpetuate human misery in order to profit therefrom politically or otherwise will encounter the opposition of the United States.

Marshall's address lasted only a few minutes. But when the plan he announced finally became a reality, America had spent $17 billion on European reconstruction and had begun a durable relationship with Western Europe. Inspired perhaps by the New Deal, the plan was also constructed out of a keen sense of the political realities and opportunities of the time and paved the way for an Atlantic security community that has brought Europe unprecedented stability. Though invited to do so, the Soviet Union declined to participate in Marshall's plan for the rebuilding of Europe.

Marshall became committed to a European recovery plan after he visited Stalin in the Soviet Union in April 1947. But, as the early papers in this book point out, a strategy for recovery in Europe had already taken shape in a number of bilateral agreements. The plan was also fashioned out of a unique procedure the Americans and Europeans created to include the Europeans in decisions about how the aid should be distributed. It was as well the first substantial step toward European reunification and a "rehearsal" for the Atlantic community.

At its best, the Marshall Plan, according to Professor Charles Maier, stood for "the belief that intelligent policy could help solve acute economic problems." The conference papers in this volume examine a wide range of questions, including whether the plan could be repeated. Most scholars represented here argue that it could not, for its success depended largely upon Europe's existing infrastructure and technically skilled population. Other scholars examine the economic and regional organizations that complemented the Marshall Plan.

The Luxembourg conference brought together men and women from government and the university. Their contributions to the success of the conference demonstrate the critical role that original ideas play in foreign and economic policy. Professor Willard Thorp, who delivered the first paper, was one of General Marshall's aides. Professor Robert Bowie helped to organize the steel and coal industries through the Schuman Plan. Herman Abs played a crucial role in Luxembourg. Professor Miriam Camps's work overlapped with that of Professor Thorp in planning at the U.S. State Department the myriad ways to put the plan into operation. Besides these contributors, other speakers at the conference said that they believed the Marshall Plan was the crucial first step in promoting cooperation among Europeans and laying the foundation for a European Common Market and a unified Europe.

The conference was an important contribution to ongoing discussions about the future of the Atlantic Alliance and the challenges of the post–Cold War era.

Dr. Armand Clesse
Special Counselor of the
  Government of Luxembourg
Luxembourg, Luxembourg

Archie C. Epps
Dean of Students in
  Harvard College
Cambridge, Massachusetts

Acknowledgments

This book includes some of the papers presented at a conference on the Marshall Plan and the building of an Atlantic community held from 17 to 22 December 1987 in Luxembourg. It was the first conference in a series organized by the Luxembourg-Harvard Association through the sponsorship of Prime Minister Jacques Santer and Dr. Armand Clesse, president of the Luxembourg-Harvard Association.

Thirty-three Harvard undergraduates attended the Marshall Plan conference, having been prepared through a rigorous seminar conducted by Harvard faculty who had taken part in the administration of the European Recovery Program or who are scholars of the period. There were over seventy European students as well. A few months after the December 1987 conference, a group of Luxembourg students visited Harvard; and several weeks later the first Harvard Model Congress Europe, a simulation of the U.S. Senate, took place at the European Convention Center in Luxembourg for two hundred high school and college students from six countries in Europe. Those activities brought to reality one of Harvard's dreams for its undergraduates: namely, that they would seize opportunities to become more sophisticated about the world and understand more fully the consequences of World War II and the Atlantic Alliance.

The collaboration between Luxembourg and Harvard grew out of a visit to Cambridge by Prime Minister Santer on the occasion of his lecture to undergraduates at Harvard College. He and his colleagues hoped to establish Luxembourg as a crossroads for the exchange of ideas among nations and between members of the university and men and women in the world of politics.

There were many who provided assistance to the conference, through both participation and financial and logistical support. Here we have to cite first and foremost the government of Luxembourg and Prime Minister Santer for his courageous and generous support. In particular, the members of the Luxembourg-Harvard Association should be singled out for their hard work and the many hours contributed to the enterprise. The members of the association besides Dr. Clesse were John Blaschette, Jules Christophory, Gaston Gengler, Jean-Marc Hoscheit, Aloys Jacoby, Jean-Jacques Kasel, Ernest Michels, and Gilbert Trausch.

Many banks and firms in Luxembourg made a financial contribution: American Bankers Club, American Luxembourg Society, Banco di Napoli International, Banco di Roma International, Banque Continentale du Luxembourg, Banque Européenne d'Investissement, Banque Générale de Luxembourg, Banque Internationale à Luxembourg, Banque de Luxembourg, Banque Nationale de Paris (Luxembourg), Banque Paribas Luxembourg, Banque U.C.L., Bayerische Landesbank International, Berliner Bank International, Caisse Centrale Raiffeisen, Caisse d'Épargne de l'État, Cedel, Commerzbank International, Compagnie Luxembourgeoise de Telediffusion, Computerland-Europe, Crédit Européen, Crédit Lyonnais, Deutsche Bank Luxembourg, Du Pont de Nemours (Luxembourg), Esso Luxembourg, Harold Gans, German Marshall Fund, Goodyear, Heintz van Landewyck, Icelandair, International Metals, Kredietbank, Société Européenne de Banque, Société Générale Alsacienne de Banque, and Paul Wurth.

The United States Embassy in Luxembourg gave a reception for the conference participants and we wish to thank in particular Ambassador Jean Girard and her staff.

We have also to acknowledge the commitment to the conference of the Harvard administration. We would especially like to thank Dean Fred Jewett and Dean Michael Shinagel. We thank especially the Harvard faculty members and others whose stimulating seminars helped prepare our undergraduates for the conference: Walter Isaacson, Milton Katz, and James Spence. And we are grateful to Laurie MacDonald, John C. MacLean, and Ellen Hatfield Towne for their editorial assistance. In Luxembourg, we would like to praise Miss Denise Schauls, who devoted many hours to conference organization and to the preparation of this manuscript.

We also acknowledge with gratitude the role of Mr. Alexander Shustorovich, a founder of the Luxembourg Colloquium while a Harvard undergraduate.

Finally, we would like to thank those in the scholarly community, in addition to the contributors to this volume, who presented lectures at the conference: Charles Maier, Giles Merritt, Jesse Man, Alan Milward, Pierre Uri, Dragoljub Najman, David Ellwood, and Robert Triffin.

Secretary of State George C. Marshall's Address at Harvard Commencement, 5 June 1947

I need not tell you that the world situation is very serious. That must be apparent to all intelligent people. I think one difficulty is that the problem is one of such enormous complexity that the very mass of facts presented to the public by press and radio make it exceedingly difficult for the man in the street to reach a clear appraisement of the situation. Furthermore, the people of this country are distant from the troubled areas of the earth and it is hard for them to comprehend the plight and consequent reactions of the long-suffering peoples, and the effect of those reactions on their governments in connection with our efforts to promote peace in the world.

In considering the requirements for the rehabilitation of Europe, the physical loss of life, the visible destruction of cities, factories, mines, and railroads were correctly estimated, but it has become obvious during recent months that this visible destruction was probably less serious than the dislocation of the entire fabric of the European economy. For the past ten years conditions have been highly abnormal. The feverish preparation for war and the more feverish maintenance of the war effort engulfed all aspects of national economies. Machinery has fallen into disrepair or is entirely obsolete. Under the arbitrary and destructive Nazi rule, virtually every possible enterprise was geared into the German war machine. Longstanding commercial ties, private institutions, banks, insurance companies, and shipping companies disappeared, through loss of capital, absorption through nationalization, or by simple destruction. In many countries, confidence in the local currency has been severely shaken. The breakdown of the business structure of Europe during the war was complete. Recovery has been seriously retarded by the fact that two years after the close of hostilities a peace settlement with Germany and Austria has not been agreed upon. But even given a more prompt solution of these difficult problems, the rehabilitation of the economic structure of Europe quite evidently will require a much longer time and greater effort than had been foreseen.

There is a phase of this matter which is both interesting and serious. The farmer has always produced the foodstuffs to exchange with the city dweller for the other necessities of life. This division of labor is the basis of modern civilization. At the present time it is threatened with breakdown. The town and city industries are not producing adequate goods to exchange with the food-producing farmer. Raw materials and fuel are in short supply. Machinery is lacking or worn out. The farmer or the peasant cannot find the goods for sale which he desires to purchase. So the sale of his farm produce for money which he cannot use seems to him an unprofitable transaction. He, therefore, has withdrawn many fields from crop cultivation and is using them for grazing. He feeds more grain to stock and finds for himself and his family an ample supply of food, however short he may be on clothing and the other ordinary gadgets of civilization. Meanwhile people in the cities are short of food and fuel (and in some places approaching the starvation level). So the governments are forced to use their foreign money and credits to procure these necessities abroad. This process exhausts funds which are

urgently needed for reconstruction. Thus a very serious situation is rapidly developing which bodes no good for the world. The modern system of the division of labor upon which the exchange of products is based is in danger of breaking down.

The truth of the matter is that Europe's requirements for the next three or four years of foreign food and other essential products—principally from America—are so much greater than her present ability to pay that she must have substantial additional help or face economic, social, and political deterioration of a very grave character.

The remedy lies in breaking the vicious circle and restoring the confidence of the European people in the economic future of their own countries and of Europe as a whole. The manufacturer and the farmer throughout wide areas must be able and willing to exchange their products for currencies the continuing value of which is not open to question.

Aside from the demoralizing effect on the world at large and the possibilities of disturbances arising as a result of the desperation of the people concerned, the consequences to the economy of the United States should be apparent to all. It is logical that the United States should do whatever it is able to do to assist in the return of normal economic health in the world, without which there can be no political stability and no assured peace. Our policy is directed not against any country or doctrine but against hunger, poverty, desperation, and chaos. Its purpose should be the revival of a working economy in the world, so as to permit the emergence of political and social conditions in which free institutions can exist. Such assistance, I am convinced, must not be on a piecemeal basis as various crises develop. Any assistance that this government may render in the future should provide cure rather than a mere palliative. Any government that is willing to assist in the task of recovery will find full cooperation, I am sure, on the part of the United States government. Any government which maneuvers to block the recovery of other countries cannot expect help from us. Furthermore, governments, political parties, or groups which seek to perpetuate human misery in order to profit therefrom politically or otherwise will encounter the opposition of the United States.

It is already evident that, before the United States government can proceed much further in its efforts to alleviate the situation and help start the European world on its way to recovery, there must be some agreement among the countries of Europe as to the requirements of the situation and the part those countries themselves will take in order to give proper effect to whatever action might be undertaken by this government. It would be neither fitting nor efficacious for the government to undertake to draw up unilaterally a program designed to place Europe on its feet economically. This is the business of the Europeans. The initiative, I think, must come from Europe. The role of this country should consist of friendly aid in the drafting of a European program and of later support of such a program so far as it may be practical for us to do so. The program should be a joint one, agreed to by a number of, if not all, European nations.

An essential part of any successful action on the part of the United States is an understanding on the part of the people of America of the character of the problem and the remedies to be applied. Political passion and prejudice should have no part. With foresight, and a willingness on the part of our people to face up to the vast responsibility which history has clearly placed upon our country, the difficulties I have outlined can and will be overcome.

I am sorry that on each occasion I have said something publicly in regard to our international situation, I've been forced by the necessities of the case to enter into rather technical discussions. But to my mind, it is of vast importance that our people reach some general understanding of what the complications really are, rather than react from a passion or a prejudice or an emotion of the moment.

As I said more formally a moment ago, we are remote from the scene of these troubles. It is virtually impossible at this distance merely by reading, or listening, or even seeing photographs or motion pictures to grasp at all the real significance of the situation.

And yet the whole world of the future hangs on a proper judg-

ment. It hangs, I think, to a large extent on the realization of the American people of just what are the various dominant factors. What are the reactions of the people? What are the justifications of those reactions? What are the sufferings? What is needed? What can best be done? What must be done? Thank you very much.

Present at the Creation

1

The Marshall Plan: A Vision and Its Implementation

JACQUES SANTER

In 1947, the Europeans faced enormous economic difficulties. Much of their industry had been destroyed. The farmers, who could not purchase anything with their produce, kept it for themselves. They had no way to buy anything outside of Europe. And the winter of 1946–47 was the harshest in many years. Agricultural production in Western Europe had reached only 83 percent of the prewar volume; industrial production 88 percent; exports scarcely 59 percent.

Also, there were nettlesome political and social problems. Some countries were shaken by endless strikes. Great Britain decided to withdraw her troops from Greece, where a merciless civil war raged. President Truman announced his aid program for democratic countries exposed to Communist subversion. But the Truman Doctrine lacked a solid base.

At the Moscow Conference in early 1947, the victorious powers could not agree about Germany. The U.S. secretary of state George Marshall feared the worst not only for Germany but for

Europe: "The patient is sinking while the doctors deliberate," he said on returning from Moscow.

On 5 June 1947 at Harvard University, commencement day, Marshall proposed an ambitious aid plan for Europe. Churchill would call it "the most unsordid act in history"; the "help for self-help" was to be offered on a basis that was not national but regional. The aid was offered to all, including the countries of Eastern Europe, even though many responsible Americans hoped secretly that the Soviet Union would reject the offer. In any case, Ernest Bevin and Georges Bidault met V. M. Molotov in Paris. The meeting failed. A second conference around mid-July brought together sixteen European countries that would more or less come to an agreement.

In December 1947, President Truman presented the European Recovery Program to Congress. Congress adopted the Economic Cooperation Act in the spring of 1948. The act planned on $5 billion for the first eighteen months of a four-year program that would ultimately cost the American people $13 billion. This represented 5 to 10 percent of the federal budget during the course of the program, or 2 percent of the U.S. gross national product. In terms of 1987, the Marshall Plan would be about equivalent to $80–100 billion.

The Marshall aid was used to buy fuel; food for people and livestock, as well as fertilizer; and machines, vehicles, and equipment.

American aid would help stabilize Western Europe and increase prosperity. Inflation would be indigenous to almost every country participating in the plan in 1950. During the period of the Marshall Plan, the global gross national product of Western Europe would increase by at least 32 percent. Agricultural production would surpass the prewar level by 11 percent, while industrial production would exceed the prewar level by 40 percent. Of course, this leap was due not only to the Marshall Plan; local resources would also play an important role in capital formation. But Marshall Plan aid would contribute the critical margin, according to Paul Hoffman (the Washington administrator of the Economic Cooperation Administration from 1948 to 1950).

Since the authors of the Marshall Plan insisted that the initiative come from participating countries and that they play a major role in their own recovery, an institution was needed that would permit joint representation. Thus was created, in Paris, the Organization for European Economic Cooperation (OEEC), which would be directed by such men as Paul Henri Spaak and Robert Marjolin. Each country would form its own recovery agency to unite agriculture and business.

The Marshall Plan was not unanimously accepted in the United States. Some argued that the Marshall Plan would increase certain deficiencies in the U.S. economy and greatly impede the United States in world affairs, and others wanted the United States to rely on fragile political coalitions devoted to democratic forms of government.

Marshall Plan aid was founded on the advantages of economic integration: an integrated economic order, consolidated by a strong central structure, would help to guide German recovery into suitable paths. It was also concerned with reestablishing the German economy and guaranteeing the security needs of its neighbors. At the same time, the Marshall Plan authors considered that such aid would help to create a sufficient force to counteract Soviet power.

The architects of the Marshall Plan also wanted to stabilize the European Union of Payments, precursor of the European Monetary System. They would depend on the Schuman Plan and the European Economic Community.

With Marshall Plan aid hardly exhausted, widely varying interpretations appeared concerning the importance of this plan and its true impact on the recovery of European economies. This diversity of views has continued, moreover, until our own day. But whatever the extent of the enterprise, the Marshall Plan greatly transformed the psychological atmosphere of Western Europe at the end of the 1940s. It restored confidence in the future to Europeans. A fundamental act of solidarity, it gave a new quality to relations between the United States and Europe and prepared the ground for a lasting commitment by Americans toward Europe. Henceforth, Americans knew that their own security could not be separated from the security and prosperity of Europe.

The Marshall Plan was a bold, unprecedented project, surpassing by far anything that had been previously thought possible. It demonstrated, as George Kennan said several months ago in Berlin, that "given the prerequisites of breadth of vision, of boldness of concept, and of determination to see the problem solved, great things could be done—great things could be done even in war-weary, sophisticated, skeptical, and in part even cynical, Europe."

The Marshall Plan was nonideological, nonadversarial, nonauthoritarian, nonpaternalistic, but rather of a practical nature, frank and cooperative. It relied on qualities such as self-determination, solidarity, partnership. It gave confidence to those who had to be helped and it respected their feelings. This approach was to characterize transatlantic relations for a long time, even if it was not always followed through.

I do not wish to minimize current economic problems such as monetary confusion, debts, budgetary deficits. But isn't it true that the tasks that confront us, in the heart of the West, are relatively modest compared to the challenge that confronted the initiators of the Marshall Plan? It is quite otherwise, of course, with the enormous problem of underdevelopment, which could certainly not be resolved by an aid program, even if it were of the extent of the European Recovery Program.

I should like to close this brief speech not on a pessimistic note, but rather on a positive one. I shall do so by evoking briefly the name of a man whose work we commemorate in part today.

General Marshall was endowed with exceptional qualities. Even his political opponents recognized his honesty, decency, simplicity, and loyalty. He cared nothing for flattering expressions, sentimental flights, or emotional effusions. When he entrusted George Kennan with spelling out the aid plan, he said simply: "Avoid trivia."

In conclusion, I should like to quote a man of a very different nature from that of George Marshall. Winston Churchill said of him in 1959:

During my long and close association with successive American administrations, there are few men whose qualities of mind and character have impressed me so deeply as those of General Marshall. He is a great American, but he is far more than that. In war he was as wise and understanding in counsel as he was resolute in action. In peace he was the architect who planned the restoration of our battered European economy and, at the same time, laboured tirelessly to establish a system of Western defense. He has always fought victoriously against defeatism, discouragement and disillusion. Succeeding generations must not be allowed to forget his achievements and his example.

2

From Marshall Plan
to a World of
Economic Interdependence

JACQUES F. POOS

Luxembourg, because it needs to look outward, lives by the rhythms of the outside world more than does any other country in Western Europe. Our national economy grows mainly by virtue of foreign investments, and our production is closely linked to the conjunctional cycles of international exchanges. But we do resemble the other eleven Western European countries insofar as we participate in a plan of economic cooperation even more integrated than the Marshall Plan: I refer to the European Economic Community (EEC).

The spirit and the political context at the heart of the 1947 Marshall Plan have deeply influenced postwar international relations, to the point of having given to Europe its current political form. This "generous offer, enlightened and efficient," as Raymond Aron called it, was, in its beginnings, designed for all European countries devastated by the worldwide conflict. Even Czechoslovakia had accepted it upon first consideration.

For the democratic European countries, the Marshall Plan was of fundamental, historic significance in terms of both economic development and regional security: For in 1948, the United States decided to remain on the continent of Europe and to assume its responsibilities in the new international system. The United States contributed directly toward the reconstruction of a democratic Europe capable of rapidly overcoming the divisions between the conquerors and the conquered. The economic and political rebirth of Western Europe was of critical importance to peace and stability. At the same time, that rebirth created the basis for a new solidarity among Europeans, a new "partnership" with the United States to guarantee Europeans security, and a balanced course of international economic development that would be profitable for all European nations.

For the four days of this conference, persons active in the Marshall Plan period both as observers and as seasoned specialists will reflect on these lessons and attempt to draw up a balance sheet on a community that, in the course of the past forty years, has demonstrated both stability and dynamism.

The Atlantic community has not aged, it has matured. It is today confronted by new challenges, but it has in the past demonstrated its resilience and adaptability to the profound changes that have shaken the world's economy and politics.

In keeping with the spirit of the Marshall Plan, we independent nations, assembled in CECA, dedicated to cooperation, have tried to extend ourselves without violating the values and convictions of any member. We know it would be folly to try, at any price, to go against such notions as "Atlantism" and "Europeanism." Six countries, now grown to twelve, aware that diffusion of their powers and energies would condemn them to a middle rank as observers of the international scene, commit themselves to internal cohesion and greater unity. The Marshall Plan and the Atlantic Alliance have contributed to European unification.

The transatlantic dialogue has in no way been diminished by the emergence of a true community of Europe. But the balance has been modified. The United States is no longer an economic giant that can afford to disregard European opinion.

Certainly, the United States occupies a primary role in the world economy. But the growing U.S. awareness of the need to compete in world markets, and of the privileged place of the dollar in the international monetary system, confer on it a new and special responsibility in the common development of international economic relations.

From this point of view, it is necessary for the Atlantic community to adapt to the new situation. Until now, the ability to adapt has clearly been part of its strength.

The signing of the Intermediate Nuclear Force (INF) Treaty, completed several days ago, illustrates this adaptive capacity. The concerted action of the Atlantic community has functioned well at every stage of a complex treaty process initiated by the famous "double-track decision" and spurred by the Reykjavik summit in October 1986. This concerted action has resulted in a historical disarmament agreement that foreshadows the complete dismantling of nuclear weapon systems installed primarily in Europe.

Everything that can reduce European tensions while preserving our common security deserves to be actively supported.

In 1947, Stalin rejected the Marshall Plan. Today, Gorbachev hopes for Western cooperation in modernizing a terminally ill Soviet economy and in raising the Soviet standard of living. This represents a remarkable historical turnabout.

But the Atlantic community must also face the challenge of returning to greater economic and monetary stability.

The October 1987 stock market crash was an abrupt and ominous warning. It indicated that the United States must take vigorous action to reduce its own sizable budget and trade deficits that, in turn, affect the world economy. The fluctuations in the dollar, which has fallen in 1986 and 1987 by more than 50 percent in relation to the principal standards, contribute to a dangerous global economic instability.

Until now, the coordination of economic policies has remained largely, despite numerous declarations, a pious wish. However, if we wish to avoid another recession that would bring greater unemployment and damage weak Third World economies, then all the partners must take responsibility and yield to a certain discipline. That is how the Atlantic community, which now includes Japan, sees the situation.

The United States cannot, as in the past, pursue a policy of "benign neglect" motivated by purely domestic considerations. And Europe, for its part, must fulfill its proper role by working for greater unity.

The economic and commercial disputes between the United States and Europe must be resolved in a unifying manner. The threat of protectionism continues to weigh on our relations at a moment when economic growth on both sides of the Atlantic demands free exchange and development of international commerce. Protectionism appears perhaps the least painful solution from an internal point of view. But its extension would quickly plunge the world economy into an economic morass all the more dangerous due to the extreme indebtedness of the Third World.

Faced with these threats to our prosperity and security, we must renew and deepen our economic international cooperation. Interdependence is today a basic datum for all economies, even that of the United States. The development of world economic balance requires economic decisionmakers to abandon outdated thinking. Interdependence calls for generous, enlightened, and effective policy.

Forty years ago, the Marshall Plan showed the way. The success has been dazzling. A devastated Europe rose from the rubble of war and the Western economies have thrived. In the same way, it is up to all of us to arrive at workable solutions to current problems.

3

The Challenge of the Marshall Plan

ARTHUR HARTMAN

With the Harvard class of 1947, I heard General George Marshall's speech at my commencement. There was another speech that day, given by T. S. Eliot. If you had polled my class, you would likely have found that we were more impressed by what T. S. Eliot had to say than by the remarks of Marshall. Part of the reason lay in Marshall's character. He had a manner of putting very important things in ways that made them sound very ordinary. It made people think that his thoughts were not terribly profound, that he was presenting something in, if I may say so, a rather American fashion of simple truth. He was also very close in character to the president of the United States, Harry Truman. Truman, in his quiet way, had a distinct influence on those around him. Truman's historical sense was what struck me the most: He realized that we had to do something in the postwar period to change the cycle of despair which had always led to conflict. Like Truman, Marshall believed that the economic issues of the postwar period had to be dealt with so as to permit the free play of political forces.

munity will exercise a collective political approach. The individual members of the community still tend to play rather independent roles in political matters.

As we look toward the future, the major problems that we will face in the West are those caused by the success of our efforts: overproduction in agriculture and the pollution that comes from industrialization. We will be challenged as to how to run industries that operate in a worldwide framework while still dependent on national legislation or, as in the case of the community, on legislation binding upon a small group of nations. What is more, we face the ethical issues that arise from the disparity between the rich and the poor nations.

We ought to look toward the future and see whether the Marshall Plan experience, and that of the entire postwar period in Europe, might not instruct us as to how to deal with problems in other areas of the globe. I think that this is the basic lesson we have learned from the Marshall Plan: The encouragement of democracy must be based on a thriving economy and on the encouragement of multinational processes that lead to creative solutions to problems.

The Challenge of the Marshall Plan

An important element of the Marshall Plan was the vi
one should use aid not only to create a new economic and
climate, but also to point the involved nations in a new
direction. In order to receive the aid, the nations had firs
to break down the economic barriers that existed betwee
The preamble of the European Recovery Program, the firs
Congress passed in furtherance of the Marshall Plan, s
that the aid should be used to promote the integration of l
In the beginning, many people had very different idea
what such integration meant. There were those, like Jea
net, who thought that it meant European unity and the
of supranational institutions. Others thought that it shoul
in a looser kind of union, one that did not require the
foreign institutions that grew out of the integration of
original recipient nations. But from the very beginning, th
an effort on the American side to use the plan not as an ec
tool but rather for political purposes, to strengthen the der
processes in Europe and the relationship between Eurc
the United States. The U.S. plan for Europe was designed
a closer community of nations that would find ways to i
their cooperation in a regional sphere and perhaps, in t
run, on a worldwide scale.

But this was not easy. The European economy had be
astated. Yet there were still trained people who knew hov
machines, businesses, and grand enterprises. There we
ernments that knew how to organize their societies.

The Marshall Plan not only restored democratic instituti
engendered economic recovery, it also confronted us w
problems of fully employed societies. It further led us t
about the role that industrialized societies could play in l
the less-developed world. The question of linking ec
recovery with institutions that would protect our securit
as NATO, also derived from the Marshall Plan.

The relative power of the United States in the world ec
has diminished. We now face a fully recovered Europe
still finding it difficult to create the institutions through v
can exercise political power. The growth in membership
Common Market has made it less likely that the Europea

4

The Origins
of the Marshall Plan

WILLARD THORP

Before World War II, many Americans believed that World War I had been a war that would end all wars. The Kellogg Pact, an international treaty renouncing war as an instrument of national policy, had been signed by sixty-three countries in 1928. In the late 1930s, Congress enacted several neutrality acts that forbade American assistance to belligerent countries.

When Hitler began his aggressions in Europe in 1936, statutory restrictions on the president and his administration were so tight that they were prevented from offering much direct assistance to the invaded countries. Secretary of State Cordell Hull asked Congress to modify the neutrality acts, but Congress refused. During the 1940 presidential campaign, both candidates pledged to keep us out of war.

The situation in Europe worsened until finally, after France and the Low Countries had been overrun, the president convinced Congress to pass the Lend-Lease Act in March 1941. This large-scale U.S. aid program set the stage for the formation of the

13

Marshall Plan. The Lend-Lease Act still maintained prohibitions against direct U.S. involvement in belligerent countries, but it did allow the United States to provide aid to combat aggressors. The aid was to be provided on a lend-lease basis, which meant that whatever amounts were used by the recipient during the war would never be charged by the United States; all amounts left unused after the war would have to be returned or paid for.

Surprisingly, Congress appropriated $9 billion for the Lend-Lease Act. The aid was primarily intended for Britain, which had exhausted its financial resources, had limited shipping, and could not do much borrowing. It looked as though Hitler would succeed unless Britain received some support. And so the Lend-Lease Act got underway with substantial shipments to Europe.

The whole situation changed with the attack on Pearl Harbor in December 1941. The United States started drafting millions of people, training them, and sending them abroad as soon as they were ready. Production was increased on an incredible scale. For example, prior to Pearl Harbor there had been but a very small U.S. aviation industry. But when President Roosevelt directed that 6,000 new airplanes be built, they were. He substantially increased the production of tanks as well. The whole country united to defeat Hitler.

Enormous amounts of U.S. exports went directly to Europe in support of our military efforts. In addition, the Lend-Lease Act provided $50 billion in products and services to the Allies: 40 percent for military equipment, 18 percent for industrial supplies, 11 percent for food, and 10 percent for motor vehicles. The largest portion of the Lend-Lease Act aid, about 62 percent, went to the British Empire. At that time, the empire included India, a colony that had been threatened by the Japanese and thus received U.S. aid through Britain. The next largest portion, 22 percent, went to the Soviet Union, which was included among the Allies after Hitler's attack on that country in June 1941. By the end of the war, the United States was conducting an enormous shipping operation based on the wide requirements of warmaking.

The Lend-Lease Act had been written to end with the war. On V-J Day, 14 August 1945, the shipments stopped. President Truman, who had voted for Lend-Lease as a senator, stood by this termination date despite pleas from some members of his administration not to end such a tremendous flow so abruptly. An agreement was finally worked out. Goods that had already been ordered could be delivered and considered a loan from the U.S. Export-Import Bank on a thirty-year basis at 2.375 percent interest, a very generous rate. In addition, goods that had been utilized by the U.S. in Europe, including automobiles and trucks, were sold on a negotiated basis.

One difficult problem in accounting and negotiation resulted from the Lend-Lease Act. Participating countries were supposed either to pay for aid materials that were not used up or to return them. Country by country, estimates were developed as to the value of goods still useful at the end of the war, and these amounts were added to other nondollar charges. There were some offsetting charges. Some countries undertook to pay the local costs associated with the Fulbright scholarship program. Some property was transferred to U.S. government ownership, thereby reducing foreign exchange payments. In the end, the Lend-Lease Act accounts were cleared at a large discount.

A new international agency, the United Nations Relief and Rehabilitation Administration (UNRRA), was established in November 1943 to ease the burden on the military of taking care of citizens in newly liberated areas. Although forty-four countries joined, the United States contributed about 75 percent of the UNRRA budget. UNRRA did everything from reviving economic activity to providing government services and taking care of refugees.

But problems arose in the UNRRA operation and the agency was finally dissolved due to conflicts with the Soviets. They felt that they had suffered the greatest damage and ought therefore to receive a tremendous percentage of the funds available in UNRRA. Although the UNRRA Council did not want to give the Soviet Union anything, on the grounds that it was an ally, the council did provide $400 million in aid to Byelorussia, a Soviet republic. But the council never received from Byelorussia what it had expected: A report on how the money was to have been spent. Between the embarrassment of having had to turn down continuing requests from the USSR and the failure of Byelorussia to meet the reporting requirements, UNRRA was gradually dismantled. But through its involvement in the Lend-Lease Act and in UNRRA, the United States gained experience in cooperation, shipping and handling, and also established a great many personal contacts in various countries.

The end of the war, however, created new problems. Europe was left in an extremely difficult situation—suffering from extensive wartime destruction, lost records, experienced personnel but no financial reserves, virtually no ships, and no easy way to earn dollars. The United States was the one place European countries could go to get substantial quantities of commodities. But the Lend-Lease Act, the lifeline to Europe, had suddenly ended.

The British had foreseen this problem. Within three weeks of the end of the war they had sent a team, which included the economist John Maynard Keynes and Lord Halifax, to Washington to discuss what they needed for the postwar period. They negotiated with Will Clayton, the undersecretary for economic affairs in the State Department, and the secretary of the treasury, Fred Vinson.

Keynes analyzed the British national picture in a two-day presentation in the Federal Reserve boardroom. Everyone in Washington who might have been involved in subsequent relief efforts was there to listen. Long negotiations followed. Keynes suggested that Britain might be able to get along with $5 billion in aid, but he wanted an additional $1 billion as a safety net. Lord Halifax seldom spoke, letting Keynes take the lead. Clayton favored a maximum of $4 billion and Vinson, behaving as treasurers usually do, suggested $3 billion. The final result, after long discussions and much use of the cables, was $3.75 billion, with an additional $700 million loan to enable Britain to settle the Lend-Lease Act account. This loan was to be paid in cash—not commodities—over fifty years at 2 percent interest with a five-year grace period at the start.

But two events virtually prevented this loan from meeting the planned purposes of reconstruction. The first was that Keynes died before being able to carry out that part of the plan having to do with blocked sterling—debts owed by the British to their colonies that had provided commodities or services on account during the war. A persuasive person, Keynes thought that he could convince these colonies that their appropriate share toward achieving the final success in the war would be to cancel these British debts. The largest debt was to India, which was on the verge of being granted independence. The British felt that they could not ask India to "pay" for that independence by forgiving the debt, and so that obligation was never canceled. Egypt, the second largest creditors, also demanded payment.

The second event arose from a provision in the Anglo-American agreement which Congress had insisted upon, namely, that the British would make the pound sterling convertible one year after they had received the loan. Committed to this stipulation, the British made the pound convertible in only eleven months. Everybody who had a pound in London dashed to the bank to turn it into dollars. There was a flood of funds moving out, and the British reserves were disappearing.

Congress was not in session during this conversion flood. Since it had formally approved the original agreement, it had to approve any alternation in the timetable. A majority of members of Congress were finally persuaded to allow some flexibility to the administration about the conversion date. Incidentally, Canada came to the aid of the British at this time by loaning over $1 billion dollars.

There were other efforts to provide badly needed funds. The Export-Import Bank was able to provide $3 billion, most of which was loaned to France, but it charged against the loan to France $600 million for the Lend-Lease account. The West Germans fared best because their relief efforts were being handled by the U.S. Army. The fund for Government and Relief in Occupied Areas (GARIOA) was paid for by the Defense Department out of its regular budget in order to keep things going.

The Swedes had an unusual problem. They had a lot of gold because they had fared well during the war. They found their gold disappearing, however, as boatloads of oranges and other imports arrived. They finally persuaded the United States not to insist on the most-favored-nation clause so that they would not see all their gold going to the United States but might instead buy from some European country in need of foreign exchange.

The Italians also applied for help, but the United States could find no easy means of giving them aid because of the complex reciprocity issues. For example, during negotiations to reduce the U.S. tariff on maraschino cherries, it was discovered that the United States had not paid adequate wages to Italian prisoners who had worked in camps in the United States during the war; a back pay agreement was ultimately reached.

Not all aid was done on a bilateral basis. The Truman administration successfully persuaded Congress to approve an appropriation called Post-UNNRA, which authorized $350 billion for use in Austria, China, Greece, and Italy. This appropriation was administered by the State Department. Then there was a separate Greek-Turkish program providing $100 million for Turkey and $300 million for Greece.

All of these demands created a cumulative tension between Congress and the administration. Members of Congress were tired of being repeatedly approached by the administration for money and of having their time taken up to deal with these problems. They wanted to know what the total final amount of aid needed would be so that they could finally settle the matter.

Congress and the administration had, in other respects, a good working relationship. State Department members were allowed to sit in with congressional committees when they were marking up a bill. They discussed many issues with members of Congress, representing the opinion of the department. Congress made it clear that one of its high priorities was to move on to reconstruction, rather than remain focused on relief efforts to keep people alive.

But Congress was only one source of pressure for a solution. The second was the Europeans themselves. Everybody from prime ministers to finance ministers would come to Washington with descriptions of the problems in their countries. They would go to Capitol Hill and tell Congress about it, creating a steady flow of European visitors, all with the same story.

People in the economic sections of the State Department were making studies of what different countries might require. Will Clayton was spending a great deal of time in Europe reporting on conditions there. I made a lot of speeches, mostly in connection with the trade field, on how the European countries could not trade with each other because they had all built up protections during the war. I emphasized that the only way to get rid of these protections was through some joint effort.

All of this ferment came into focus when General George Marshall became secretary of state. Marshall had always been a military man; he was in the army until he retired at sixty-five. He rose to chief of staff during the war, meaning that he was the president's man. He was in charge of all the other generals, including Patton and Eisenhower.

Just after Marshall happily retired in November 1945, Truman asked him to go to China to work out some sort of settlement between Chiang Kai-shek and Mao. Within a week, Marshall was on a ship to China. Within another month, he had virtually negotiated a cease-fire. He was so confident about it that he returned to report all details to Truman, but when he got back to China the fighting had broken out again. He called on the individual generals scattered around China and tried to line them all up, but there were just too many of them. He would get half of China quieted down and the other half would start fighting again. He finally informed the president that he was not able to achieve a settlement among the parties.

When Marshall again returned to Washington, he received an unexpected notice that he was now to be secretary of state. Again, he was put in an unfamiliar situation. He knew many people in Washington as he had been stationed there during the war, but he had never been connected with the State Department but for his role in distant China.

Soon after assuming his new post, Marshall attended a Council of Foreign Ministers meeting in Moscow where accumulated differences on German policy were discussed. Several weeks later, Marshall came back from this meeting distressed that he could not seem to get anywhere with the Soviets in dealing with the division of Germany.

Before he left for the council meeting, he suggested that George Kennan prepare a detailed memorandum on the economic and political situation in Europe. Kennan assembled whatever was available from many different people and departments. Charles

Bohlen was then given the memorandum and prepared it in the form of a speech. Marshall then worked over the draft of the speech and discussed it with Truman. He delivered the speech at the Harvard commencement exercises on 5 June 1947.

This eight-minute speech was the impetus for the Marshall Plan. Simple, direct, and matter-of-fact, it was neither emotional nor complicated. The ideas it pulled together came from many individuals, and they emerged in the context of an international crisis.

The first half of the speech dealt with the European situation and came mostly from Clayton's work. The second half contained the key contribution: the decision that it was up to Europe to come up with a plan and that, if it did, the United States would support it. While the speech was clearly written, it did not indicate numbers or names; Marshall proposed to involve only those countries willing to join in the common plan.

Everyone knew what the problems were, but no one—until that speech—had placed responsibility for a common solution upon the European countries. Who was responsible for this key contribution? Marshall certainly was the final author, but not in the sense that he started scribbling on a piece of paper. The State Department does not work that way. Sometimes three alternative speeches are drafted. Other times, the final speaker himself works thoroughly over these drafts. This speech is so like Marshall that he must have had the major hand in it.

After the speech was given, the first question was how Europe would react. On 16 June, Georges Bidault, the dapper French foreign minister, and Ernest Bevin, the British foreign minister and labor organizer of more than average size, met in Paris. When the conference between this odd couple broke down, they asked V. I. Molotov to join them in order to determine if the USSR wished to join. Molotov accepted the invitation and made this proposal: The United States should be asked how much money it would give, that amount should be divided by country, and each country should go its own way with its share of the total. When Bidault and Bevin replied that his suggestion was not a *common* plan, Molotov decided that the Soviet Union would not join.

Many people had expected this response. The Soviets were not joiners; they had declined previous invitations to participate in cooperative efforts. Cooperation would take away some of their freedom and especially their privacy. It would necessitate giving information about their private affairs. It would require team planning. The Soviets' reasoning here reflected the problems the Allies had experienced with them during the war as to discussions of military strategy; their reasoning was also similar to that of Byelorussia in failing to report how it had spent its $400 million.

Marshall's speech made possible the Marshall Plan, but it took a great deal of effort to get from one to the other. The speech required the Europeans to prepare and to present an overall plan for Europe's recovery. Sixteen countries joined in creating the Organization for European Economic Cooperation (OEEC). Discussions began at once. Not only did each country have to make up its own plan, but each had to create a European plan with a grand total figure. It was a great achievement that, by September 1947, each country presented the U.S. government with a four-year program that included an import deficit of over $22 billion as well as additional proposals for reducing obstacles to trade among themselves. During this interim period, Congress authorized the State Department to provide $540 million worth of food, feed, and fertilizer to Austria, France, Italy, and China.

The Truman administration recognized that the proposed program was a major break from the U.S. isolationist past, and that it would not be easy. As of the time of Marshall's speech, there had been neither staff assigned to prepare the necessary legislation nor even funds appropriated for planning. The job was done by borrowing personnel from many agencies and by having regular duties covered by already overloaded colleagues. Regular hours were often disregarded. Truman set up three high-powered cabinet-level committees, one to report on Europe's needs, another on the availability of raw materials, and the third on the probable effect on the U.S. economy. A Citizen's Committee for the Marshall Plan undertook to educate the public.

A proposed act was sent to Congress on 19 December 1947; hearings began twenty days later. Senator Arthur Vandenberg was the lead-off speaker in the Senate; there were nine government witnesses, eighty-six other witnesses, and seventy-six written communications. The Senate hearings filled 1,449 pages and the House hearings added 2,269 pages more. There were endless executive sessions on the details of the legislation. It was miraculous that the Foreign Assistance Act was passed and signed on 3 April 1948. This authorization was followed by the Foreign Aid Appropriation Act of 1948, which provided funds for the first year of the plan. The administration had to appear before Congress each year thereafter for a general review in order to assure congressional appropriation for the next year. The president nominated Paul Hoffman to serve as administrator of the plan.

One step remained. Congress had required that each recipient country should sign a bilateral agreement with the United States in which each nation would agree both to a statement of policy and to procedural requirements set forth largely in the Foreign Assistance Act. Hoffman was allowed to start making shipments, but the shipments were to end if the bilateral agreements were not in effect by 3 July 1948. The agreements were reached just in time. Fourteen countries had signed immediately; the others had to wait until their parliaments could act.

The Marshall Plan was now in place. It called for the creation of a new European organization, the OEEC, and a new U.S. organization, the European Recovery Administration. It provided for the authorization and appropriation of funds by the U.S. government. Basic objectives and procedures were set forth to assure cooperation between Europe and the United States. Finally, the Marshall Plan had won popular support on both sides of the Atlantic.

5

Economics and Other Developments in the Era of the Marshall Plan

ROBERT BOWIE

It is important to understand the context in which the Marshall Plan, the European community, and the North Atlantic Treaty Organization (NATO) were created between 1947 and 1955. A revolutionary change occurred during that time in the approach both to keeping peace and to assuring economic prosperity, two of the most important goals of any nation. The Allies had done a lot of planning on these topics during the war and had agreed on measures that were supposed to achieve these purposes.

The Allied plans were based essentially on two premises. The first—and most central—premise was that the three major victors, the United States, Britain, and the Soviet Union, would cooperate in the postwar period to maintain the peace and to achieve prosperity. The second premise was that Europe would be able to recover quickly from the wartime devastation once a global free-trade economic system was in place.

Several institutions and programs were established on the basis of these premises. The United Nations, established to keep the peace and to provide security, was one of the most important of these. The Security Council was its main instrument; China, France, and the three major victors each had veto power over the council's decisions.

The victors agreed to prevent Germany and Japan from becoming a threat in the future by keeping them disarmed, weak, and under control. Nevertheless, they had decided to treat Germany as a single economic unit because of its importance to the health of the European economies. Finally, the powers proposed an open trading system based on the General Agreement on Tariffs and Trade (GATT), the World Bank, and the International Monetary Fund. They hoped that this system would provide a framework within which all countries of the world, including those countries that were becoming independent as a result of the breakup of the colonial system, could find a place.

In the period following 1945, however, mounting evidence suggested that these premises were not valid and that the policies based on them were not working. This awareness developed gradually both in Europe and in the United States, crystallizing around 1947 when the Marshall Plan was adopted.

The first sign that these premises were incorrect involved the wartime allies. Not only was the Soviet Union not cooperating in the way the other allies had hoped, it had become a threat. Its noncooperation was evident in Iran in 1946; in the steady imposition of Communist regimes in Eastern Europe; and in the uprisings in Greece and Turkey, which were thought to be at least partially induced or supported by the Soviet Union. There were also the failure of the postwar conferences, including one in Moscow in April 1947 from which Marshall came back totally disillusioned with the possibility of arriving at agreements. Finally, there was a breakdown of cooperation in the Allied Control Council, which was supposed to regulate the revival of Germany. The treatment of Germany as a single economic unit, vital in making the German economy work, was blocked.

The second sign that the premises had been faulty was that Europe was not recovering, but rather stagnating. Not only

Europe's physical assets, but also its entire infrastructure, had been destroyed. The operation of these economies had been so undermined that they simply could not get going again, even with substantial, albeit piecemeal, contributions from the United States.

Because the Soviet Union had failed to cooperate in carrying out the plans for Germany, the United States and Britain, and ultimately France, were forced to develop a program for putting their zones of Germany together. They created first Trizonia, which developed later into the Federal Republic of Germany.

Although it was evident that what had been planned and put in place was not working, it was not clear what should be done instead. The effort to hammer out agreements among the Western nations resulted in extensive debate on a number of major issues. There was indeed recognition of the necessity to respond to the problems, but there was no obvious or inevitable way to respond.

Neither was the problem itself neatly defined. For example, there was a wide divergence of opinion as to how much of a threat the Soviet Union posed. As time went on, these different views became more explicit. In February 1946, Kennan made an extensive analysis of Soviet purposes that he published one year later, in the July 1947 edition of *Foreign Affairs*, under the pseudonym Mr. X and entitled "The Sources of Soviet Conduct." His unsentimental analysis was essentially that the Soviet Union would not cooperate, and indeed was engaged in a hostile contest with the West. At about the same time, Churchill spoke publicly for the first time of the divisive "iron curtain" that the Soviet Union had lowered in Eastern Europe. On the other hand, various people in the United States and Europe disputed this analysis of Soviet purposes.

When questions arose about the U.S. role in Europe's defense, or about the structure of Europe, there was a great deal of debate in Congress, and across the Atlantic as well. When Robert Schuman proposed the European integration plan prepared by Jean Monnet, the British were absolutely opposed. Not only did they not want to take part, but for a period they tried to head it off.

Difficult questions arose as to the strategy and size of forces necessary for the defense of Europe, the actual capabilities of NATO, the extent of justifiable reliance upon nuclear weapons, and the role conventional weapons should play. Discussions also ensued as to what various countries should be prepared to pay for defense, given the other claims on their resources in this difficult period. Perhaps the most divisive issue concerned whether and how Germany would be rearmed.

In addition to these problems, there were radical changes both with respect to Europe's own structure and to relations among the United States, Europe, and the Soviet Union. Much of what had been agreed upon only a few years before was overturned simply because it was not working.

Remarkably, what was done was not simply ad hoc. The tendency of governments when faced with a problem, particularly an awkward, unfamiliar one for which they are not really prepared, is to muddle through. But in the case of postwar European recovery, a strategic point of view was employed and fundamental questions were asked. The result was the formation of a set of relationships which has endured and kept the peace for forty years. It was a remarkable achievement, almost miraculous as regards governmental policymaking, because it involved the cooperation of more than a dozen democratic countries, each with different perspectives, needs, and motivations.

Marshall returned from the 1947 Moscow conference convinced that the Soviet Union was trying to prevent solutions in the postwar conferences in the hope that turmoil and disruption in Western Europe would make it an easy target for Communist takeover. After all, there were already powerful Communist parties in Italy and France, each holding positions in the government. The Marshall Plan was intended to make it possible for these countries to gain sufficient economic stability to follow a course of their own choosing. If they were able to do so, they would not be easy marks, despite their domestic turmoil, for a Communist takeover. This worry was not unfounded: Soviet pressure on Czechoslovakia had already resulted in a Communist seizure of power.

Undoubtedly, there was an anti-Communist component to the Marshall Plan. Nevertheless, there was also a bona fide proposal to the Soviets and their satellite countries to join. While there were some qualms about what the consequences might be, the offer was genuine. The Soviets drew back because they were not prepared to provide the information or to submit themselves to the inevitable discipline of the kind of program being proposed.

The second stage of development of these new institutions, which changed the direction of policy, was the evolution of NATO. It began with a European initiative in the Benelux Treaty, but quickly became a proposal for U.S. participation in the Atlantic Alliance. Initially, U.S. involvement was seen only as a guarantee; there were no expectations of any substantial U.S. forces being sent over to Europe. Minimal U.S. occupation forces were stationed in Europe, but they were not effective fighting forces. The assumption was that the United States would only become involved if there were a war in Europe. The U.S. commitment was expected to be enough to deter any possibility of invasion. Indeed, there was no serious expectation, before the Korean invasion, that the Soviets were about to invade and march to the English Channel. The concern then was subversion assisted by the predominant strength of the Soviet Union and its proximity— just on the other side of the Iron Curtain. The U.S. guarantee was meant to reassure the Europeans that they could safely go about the business of trying to create the kind of societies they might want without fear of internal takeover.

By June 1950, however, everything changed. The invasion of Korea led to new concerns about the possibility of an invasion of Western Europe. Facile parallels were drawn between Korea and Germany: both countries were divided, and just beyond the borders of both were substantial Communist forces. This fear led the Europeans, in September 1950, to request the stationing in Europe of a substantial number of U.S. forces and the appointment of a U.S. commander for NATO. The integrated NATO force was looked upon as necessary to deterrence and resistance. A U.S. commander was thought of as both symbolic and a possible means of engaging U.S. nuclear weapons in the defense of Europe. The United States agreed with most of this plan, but insisted that a way be found to bring West Germany into NATO as a participant in its own defense. (This issue proved divisive for several years until it was resolved in 1955.)

Just before the issue of German NATO participation arose, however, Schuman had put forward a proposal, prepared by Monnet, for the European Coal and Steel Community. The idea of a united Europe was not new; it had been discussed for some years, but never on a practical level. The practical significance of Schuman's plan was twofold. First, it narrowed the initial field of integration to coal and steel, both critical industries for peace and war. Second, its radically different approach to Germany sought reconciliation in order to avoid future civil wars in Europe and to end the isolation of Germany.

This was, after all, only five years after a harsh, cruel, devastating war. The French, who had suffered humiliation and hardships, had been in the forefront of those insisting that Germany be controlled. They called for its supervision by an international authority that would assure that Germany did not exploit the coal and steel markets, and also by a variety of administrative boards to keep them disarmed. France was determined to prevent the Germans from becoming a threat.

It became apparent to Schuman that these controls were gradually eroding due both to the threat from the Soviet side and to the necessity of forming Trizonia and thus creating some sort of a West German regime. (The latter necessity had been met in 1949 by the formation of the Federal Republic and the election of Konrad Adenauer.) Schuman recognized that the French were, by their efforts to keep controls on Germany, in danger of becoming isolated.

There was an idealistic element to Schuman's thinking. He feared that history would simply repeat itself if a concept like that of the Treaty of Versailles—holding the Germans down—was perpetuated. Schuman concluded that there needed to be a radically different approach toward reconciliation. The situation was ripe for his proposal because even those who had been in the French Resistance and hated the Germans agreed that reconciliation had to be achieved in order to avoid civil wars in Europe.

A second purpose of Schuman's proposal was to gain eventually the benefits of a large market. In addition, the Europeans so depended on the United States, and the United States was so dominant, that many people felt Europe had to unite in order to regain some control over its own destiny in foreign affairs and policymaking.

Schuman took a bold and courageous step in advocating these changes at a time when feelings from the war still ran high. Many people were still suffering from the way the Germans had conducted the war and the subsequent Nazi occupations. The success of the negotiations was remarkable, considering these complications and the novelty of the proposal.

The credit goes primarily to Schuman for taking the initiative and to Adenauer for immediately clasping the outstretched hand. But the negotiators, Monnet and Walter Hallstein, were also important players. They saw the common problems and set out to create a system that would furnish common rules and institutions fundamental to a multinational organization.

During the 1950s, the British were hostile to this approach. They still labored under illusions about their role in the world. These illusions were understandable, but certainly not helpful. The British had been on the winning side in the war and had behaved courageously. Their delusions of grandeur stemmed as well from overestimating the significance of the commonwealth and of their "special relationship" with the United States. Hence, they were convinced that Britain could play a global role larger than was justified by its own strength. That expectation made Britain a disruptive factor in the European community.

The progress toward European integration was soon complicated by efforts to rearm Germany. The French opposed the establishment of a German national army. Using the community idea as a basis for a common European army, they proposed in October 1950 the Plevan Plan, which ultimately developed into the European Defense Community treaty. After a long struggle, the French rejected the treaty in 1950, even though they had originally proposed it. Finally, an alternate solution allowed Germany to participate both in the Western European Union (with some restraints) and in NATO (as a full member). The underlying problem was relations with the Soviet Union. That task was complicated when the U.S. nuclear monopoly was broken by the Soviet Union at about this time. The Soviets tested their first weapon in 1949 and several years later tested a hydrogen weapon.

These developments shed a whole new light on the consequences of warfare.

Early on in his administration, Eisenhower reached the conclusion that nuclear war would be a disaster that had to be avoided. At the same time, he felt that, with the inability of the Europeans to put up enough forces for an effective conventional defense, there was no way, under the NATO deterrence strategy, to avoid relying heavily on nuclear weapons.

Then came the death of Stalin in 1953, and the jockeying over the succession. By 1955, the Soviets themselves began to speak in similar terms about nuclear war—first G. M. Malenkov and then N. S. Khrushchev allowed that it would be suicidal and hence must be avoided.

Khrushchev formulated the Soviet doctrine of "peaceful coexistence," which he defined to mean that relations between the two sides must be conducted in such a way as to avoid any nuclear war, while allowing for continued struggle and rivalry. He made the rivalry quite explicit by intensifying the effort to expand Soviet influence through other means. Khrushchev shifted the focus, once there was a balance within Europe through NATO, to the periphery, or outlying regions, and in particular to the new countries that he saw as fertile ground for the Soviet system. He thought that the Soviet Union could be held out as a model, and that the new countries would reject capitalism and be drawn to communism.

By 1955, the situation in Europe had been largely stabilized. Western Europe had been organized in important ways, militarily through NATO and economically in the Organization for Economic Cooperation and Development (OECD) arrangements and in the emerging community. The Marshall Plan had made an important contribution toward that progress. Stability and cooperation in Western Europe and close working arrangements between Europe and the United States have been basic to European security and prosperity for nearly forty years.

6

The Marshall Plan and European Economic Integration

MIRIAM CAMPS

If one looks at the state of European economic integration today, what does one see? Very briefly: a European community, which is based on the treaties establishing the European Coal and Steel Community, Euratom (the European atomic energy authority), and the Common Market. This community, recently supplemented by the European Single Act, has grown from its original six members to twelve, with a number of other countries actively considering membership. Most other Western European countries, as well as many former colonies of the member countries, are linked to the community by trade arrangements ranging from free-trade areas to preferential arrangements that would have difficulty meeting the tests of Article 24 of the General Agreement on Tariffs and Trade (GATT). In this economic community, the Council of Ministers, still acting in important cases by unanimity, is the dominant institution. The council has become more, rather

31

than less, important relative to the European Economic Commission as the years have passed, contrary to the expectations of the founding fathers.

The commission, which is now composed of seventeen men—no woman has yet served on it—is an unwieldy body, and its current members are, for the most part, less impressive than were many of their predecessors. The commission is less a "supranational" body than was the High Authority of the Coal and Steel Community in its early days, and it is less influential than was the Hallstein Commission in the first years of the Common Market. The staff of the commission has lost much of the élan that characterized it in the early days and, perhaps inevitably, it shows some signs of bureaucratic entropy.

The European Assembly is now called the European Parliament and is directly elected, but it still has negligible power. Perhaps the Court of Justice is the only institution that has developed as the authors of the founding treaties envisaged.

The European Economic Community is a customs union with a fairly low external tariff and a common commercial policy. It also has an expensive common agricultural policy that almost everyone knows needs radical change. The internal market is gradually being freed from the many forms of government action—such as subsidies—which distort competition even after tariffs have been eliminated. This process is supposed to be completed by 1992. Some, but not all, of the community countries belong to the European Monetary System (EMS). This has been useful in providing a measure of stability to the currencies of its members, but the EMS has not yet developed into the European Monetary Union many had hoped it would. In addition, there are various European projects for collaboration in space and advanced technology. Some of these are linked to the community.

Regular political discussions among foreign ministers are now an accepted part of community life, and staff arrangements have been set up in all the member countries to support them. The whole is now crowned by the European Council of Ministers, who are heads of state or government. The meetings of the council, however, have tended to produce headlines in which "deadlock" appears more often than "breakthrough."

This thumbnail sketch of today's community may be somewhat unflattering, but it is not far wrong. Against it must be set the fact that there clearly is a new and growing relationship among the member countries which is recognized by members and nonmembers alike. The community is not just another international organization. It is an important participant in the international scheme of things, though it plays a role that is hard to define and varies with each issue. In short, although what exists is important and unique, the community of the 1980s is far from being the federal or quasifederal entity that was talked about in the heady days of the early 1950s. Back then, expressions such as the "United States of Europe" were used seriously.

Given the nature of European integration today, it is reasonable to ask whether something similar might not have evolved within the Organization for European Economic Cooperation (OEEC), established in 1948 in the context of the Marshall Plan and the forerunner of today's Organization for Economic Cooperation and Development (OECD). Or, to put the question slightly differently, the Schuman Plan, the long struggle over the European Defense Community (EDC), the difficult negotiations on the Treaties of Rome, the frequently acrimonious and ultimately unsuccessful negotiations on a European free-trade area in the 1950s, and the unsuccessful accession negotiations between the British and the "six" (Belgium, France, Italy, Luxembourg, the Netherlands, and West Germany) in the early 1960s—were they all in some way necessary to arrive at what we see today? One could debate this question for a long time and arrive at no consensus. But it may be illuminating to look briefly at three specific aspects of the question:

1. Could the OECC have evolved into the European community we see today?

2. If they had ended in success rather than failure, could the free-trade–area negotiations that took place in 1956–58 have led to much the same kind of European community as we have today?

3. Had the first British negotiations for accession not been

vetoed by General Charles de Gaulle in January 1963, would the community today be appreciably different?

Despite the fact that today's community falls far short of what many Europeans, as well as their American supporters, had originally hoped for, it is still a far more integrated community than any arrangement that would have resulted from the OEEC as it took shape in the late 1940s.

When the essential elements of the Marshall Plan were first being worked out in the summer of 1947, after Marshall's Harvard speech, Will Clayton, the U.S. undersecretary for economic affairs, met with Western European leaders and pressed them to add a commitment to the formation of a customs union to their originally proposed program. But the British, Scandinavians, and Swiss refused, and the OEEC charter contained no such commitment. Later, during the period of Marshall aid, other pressures were brought to bear on the British by the United States, by other members of the OEEC, and by the OEEC secretary general Robert Marjolin to agree to measures that might have led to the formation of a customs union. Although the British were prepared to remove quantitative restrictions on trade and to be active participants in the OEEC Steering Board for Trade, they argued that they could not contemplate membership in a European customs union and that action on tariffs should remain the province of the GATT.

Strong British resistance to having the OEEC work on customs union questions is not the only reason for concluding that the route through the six, rather than an evolution of the OEEC, was necessary. In those years, France was a very protectionist country; the need for high tariffs was an article of faith for its government, industry, and trade unions, and France was the problem country in the OEEC program for quota removal. Few Frenchmen then believed that the stimulus of freer trade would be good for French industry.

The appeal of the Schuman Plan was not that it created a free-trade area in a few segments of industry, but that it offered a way around the difficult problem of Germany. It gave France an acceptable way to agree to the revival of the coal and steel resources of the Ruhr and the ending of discrimination against

German production which had been inherent in the International Authority for the Ruhr. In addition, it gave the Germans an alternative to reunification and held out the promise of a new relationship between France and Germany, which, in Schuman's words, would make war between them unthinkable. Although, in time, West Germany would have been accepted by its European neighbors on a basis of equality, the process would have been slower without the drama of the Schuman Plan and the visions of building the United States of Europe.

The proposed EDC and the associated European Political Community went too far too fast and were both rejected by the French Assembly. But a new relationship between France and Germany had been given substance by the Schuman Plan, and this new relationship was an essential condition precedent to the two Treaties of Rome that established Euratom and the Common Market a few years later. During the Common Market negotiations, just as during the negotiations in the Steering Board for Trade in the OEEC, France was the country that posed the most difficulties and to which others made the most concessions. Robert Marjolin's recently published memoir gives many details of the widespread French opposition, not just from the Patronat and the trade unions, but from much of the French administration as well, to the formation of the Common Market. It is unlikely that the negotiations on the Common Market would have succeeded had it not been for French recognition of the importance of the new relationship with Germany and the political aura that attached to the building of the community of six.

There are other reasons, too, for thinking that the detour via the six was a necessary route to today's community of twelve. By the early 1950s, the Korean War was shifting American concern from European integration to rearmament. Then, as the European countries grew stronger and the pound and other currencies were being made convertible, those in the U.S. administration who had always preferred global trade and payment arrangements to regional ones would probably have prevailed over those who had argued for special intra-European arrangements. The time when the United States would not only welcome, but actively encourage, an OEEC effort to form a

Europeanwide customs union was coming to an end, giving way to concern with the increased discrimination against American exports inherent in any such scheme.

Finally, the essential reason the British began to reexamine their economic and political relationship with Europe was the existence of the Common Market.

In short, without the perhaps unrealistic visions of Jean Monnet and other "Europeans" of the early 1950s, it is doubtful that there would have been a European community of six. And had there been no Common Market established by the six in the late fifties, it is unlikely that there would be a community of twelve today.

The second question posed above was whether the negotiations on a OEEC-wide free-trade area which took place in 1957–58, if they had resulted in agreement rather than failure, might have led to much the same kind of community as we see today. Again, the answer is almost certainly no.

In June 1955, at Messina, the foreign ministers of the six formally resolved to establish a Common Market and agreed on the procedures to be followed in working out a detailed plan. Following the Messina conference, an intergovernmental committee was established, presided over by Henri Spaak, the Belgian foreign minister. It met throughout the summer and early autumn. A British representative participated in these discussions, but he did so without any commitment from the British government to the objective the others had accepted: the formation of a general common market.

In November 1955, the British representative left the Spaak Committee discussions. Views differ as to whether he was withdrawn or asked to leave. Probably the best description is that Spaak opened the door and the British representative walked through it. At that time, Spaak wanted only those governments that had accepted the objective of a common market to continue to participate in the work, and the British were not yet prepared to give that commitment. The British government accepted the view that it could not join a European customs union, partly because of its arrangements with the commonwealth and partly because it was not prepared to accept the pressures toward further integration implicit in a customs union. Rather surprisingly, it was not until after the British representative left the Spaak Committee that there was any real consideration by the British cabinet of the implications for Britain of the plans then being discussed among the six.

For a brief period at the end of 1955, the British tried to stop the six from going ahead by pointing out the damage that would be done to relations in the OEEC and elsewhere. At that time, many of those most closely concerned with these questions believed that the Common Market plan would fail without British participation. Indeed, this view was held even by some leading figures in the six. The forthright British statement of opposition to the plan did not lessen the determination of the six, as some had apparently anticipated, but rather made the six more determined to press ahead with their own plans. It also made them view with suspicion later British attempts to come to terms with them.

The period of outright hostility toward the Common Market was short-lived, and by the spring of 1956 the British indifference and antagonism to the plans of the six had given way to a more positive examination of the position to be adopted. From this examination emerged the idea of linking the customs union of the six with a free-trade area in which Britain and other OEEC countries would participate.

In both customs unions and free-trade areas, participating countries eliminate quotas and tariffs on trade with one another, but in a customs union a common tariff and a common commercial policy are adopted toward countries outside the union. In a free-trade area each country can maintain its own tariff and pursue its own commercial policy vis-à-vis nonmember countries.

The free-trade area the British had in mind extended only to industrial products. By excluding agriculture and keeping control over their own tariffs on non-European trade, they would be able to have free trade with the European countries without jeopardizing in any serious way their arrangements with the commonwealth. They could also continue their own system of agricultural support, which was totally different from the continental systems. And this looser arrangement would also have few built-in pressures toward further integration.

The predominant view among the Europeans who believed most strongly in European integration was, and still is, that the British, by proposing the free-trade area, were deliberately seeking to destroy the Common Market. There was much talk about the lump of sugar being dissolved in the cup of tea; the Common Market was the lump of sugar and the free-trade area the cup of tea. In particular, there was concern that by holding forth the prospect of free trade without the other commitments to common policies and to various other restrictions on freedom of action which were envisaged in the Treaty of Rome, Dr. Ludwig Erhard and his friends would prevail in Germany and the free-trade area would, in the end, supplant the Common Market. Perhaps that would have been the result, but at the time the British proposed the free-trade area, the implications of trying to marry the two schemes had not been thought through. At the start, there was much support from leaders within the six for the free-trade area as a way of bringing the British into closer association with the Common Market. It was only later that the difficulties and dangers of linking the two became apparent. Although the dissolution of the Common Market was not the primary motive behind the free-trade area proposal, the British *did* want to have the best of both worlds: an arrangement that would allow their industrial goods to compete in the markets of the six on equal terms, while preserving an almost free hand to continue their trading arrangements with the commonwealth.

The free-trade–area proposal involved no basic political "choice" on the part of the British government. Nevertheless, it did represent a shift in the British government's attitudes and marked the beginning of the questioning of the priorities that had, before that time, conditioned official thinking about Britain's external relationships. Europe began to move up the scale, the commonwealth to move down, and the nature of Britain's relationship with the United States to come into truer perspective: perspective that gave greater weight to the power disparity between the United States and Britain, which had been to some

extent obscured in the first few years after the war by the lingering effect of the wartime partnership between the two countries.

After long negotiations in the Maudling Committee, the British
agreed to some harmonization of tariffs and to other measures
that, though not as far-reaching as the commitments the six were
then prepared to accept in the Common Market, would probably
have set up pressures leading the participants closer to a customs
union than had been envisaged in the original British proposal.
It is not, therefore, as unreasonable as it might at first appear to
ask whether a successful outcome to the Maudling Committee
negotiations in 1958 might not have been a shortcut to the current
community. But again the answer is no.

The free-trade–area negotiations aroused new British industrial
interest in continental markets and forced the government to look
at the commonwealth in new ways, opening the door to the formation of new policies. The long negotiations created strains
within the six, but they also led them to go further and faster in
the creation of the Common Market than they might otherwise
have gone. For the six could not logically argue that the free-
trade areas, as envisaged by the British, did not have strong
enough institutions and common policies unless they were willing to adopt such measures themselves.

Although the threat of the free-trade area probably solidified
the six and made their external tariff lower than it might otherwise have been, the actual process of trying to establish a free-
trade–area link before the Common Market was firmly established would probably have slowed the progress of the six at a
critical time. Also, the kind of arrangement that might eventually
have been agreed to would probably have been a bad arrangement for outsiders. Not only would there have been little incentive for the six to have a moderate external tariff, but also the
policymaking process for dealing with outsiders would have been
incredibly complicated. British thinking about their European role
had not progressed far enough for them to take an effective lead
in steering a complicated two-tier system, and the six were not
yet cohesive enough to do so. Thus, a successful outcome to the
Maudling Committee negotiations might well have led, not to

today's community of twelve, but to the eventual disintegration of both the free-trade area and the Common Market.

It is also important to remember that in the spring of 1958, General Charles de Gaulle had returned to power. He was no admirer of the Common Market. The critical decisions on the devaluation of the franc and on the reorganization of French finances which made it possible for the French to take the first substantive steps, as required by the Treaty of Rome, on 1 January 1959 had still to be made. The French halt to the negotiations on the free-trade area in November 1958 may well have bought time for the Common Market at a crucial point.

The third question posed above concerned the first British negotiations for accession to the community that were halted by de Gaulle's veto in January 1963. Had these negotiations succeeded, would the structure of Europe be appreciably different today?

The answer to this question differs from the answer to the first two. The pace of development probably would not have been much different had the British joined the community in 1963 or 1964 instead of a decade later; the general shape of the community would probably be much the same as it is today, although some particular aspects might well be different. Indeed, some of the differences might be improvements. This is not to say that the British were committed "Europeans" in the 1960s. They were not. The dominant arguments used by the government were commercial ones, and the reasons for joining were frequently expressed in double negatives: "We cannot afford to stay out." But the government of Prime Minister Harold Macmillian knew it was taking a decisive political step for essentially political reasons. Moreover, during the eighteen months that elapsed between the application and the veto, the British position evolved considerably, as it had during the earlier Maudling Committee negotiations.

By 1963, the Common Market was fully established. The first steps toward the formation of the customs union had been taken well ahead of the schedule set down in the treaty. In the 1960s, the threat to the existence of the community did not come from outside, as it had in the 1950s, but from within, as de Gaulle demonstrated during the 1965 crisis over the commission's proposals on financing agricultural policy. For six months, the French pursued an empty-chair tactic, not participating in most discussions of the community. The commission had unwisely tried to force the pace of integration by linking financial arrangements on agriculture which were advocated by the French to an increase in its own power and that of the European Assembly. But had the crisis not occurred at that time, it is likely that another opportunity would have been sought by de Gaulle to throw sand in the works, both to slow down (or halt) the process of *engrenage* and to prevent the move to majority voting that the Treaty of Rome stipulated should take place in 1966.

Had the British become members of the Common Market in late 1963 or early 1964, the pace of integration would undoubtedly have been slower than the commission and the strongest Europeans would have liked. But British participation would not have made much more difference, for de Gaulle was determined to slow down the process in any case. The heady days of the Common Market, the days when things were moving quickly, had passed. Had the British been on the inside in 1965, the commission probably would not have tried to force the pace, but had it done so the French would not have dared to pursue an empty-chair policy lest the British and the Germans come together and outmaneuver them. Something like the Luxembourg compromise would probably have emerged, given the similarity between the French and British views on majority voting. It is probable that a common agricultural policy, closer to the continental system than to the British system, would have been adopted at first. But the agricultural policy might well have developed over the years into a less protectionist arrangement than it is today, for the configuration would have been different.

The hurdles the British had to leap to join the community in the early 1970s were considerably higher than those of the previous decade. The "terms of entry" that were in outline in 1963, when the veto was imposed, would not have brought forth as much domestic opposition in Britain as did the terms that had to be accepted in the seventies. Had the British joined in the mid-sixties, there might have been long and acrimonious debates over budget questions, but they would have taken a different form from those debates that later soured relationships, because the British would not have been trying to change a system already negotiated among the six.

The main reason it would have been better for Britain, for the continental countries, and for third countries like the United States if the accession negotiations in the early sixties had succeeded is that the economic situation was immeasurably better in the early sixties than it was a decade later. Difficult adjustments are more easily made in periods of expansion and optimism than in times of contraction and uncertainty. The seventies were characterized by oil embargoes and dramatic oil price increases, "Nixon shocks" (the abrupt U.S. measures taken in August 1971 to impose an import levy and to shut the gold window), the disintegration of crucial aspects of the postwar international monetary system, and a bewildering combination of inflation and stagnation.

By the late sixties and early seventies, the high importance that the U.S. government had earlier attached to the process of European integration had given way to skepticism. For some people, the building of Europe now seemed unnecessary; in the jargon of the day, the European community had become "obsolete." For most people—in the United States and in Europe—the process had become rather boring; it was still useful, but it was no longer important enough to override competing national interests. The U.S. government was no longer prepared to exchange economic disadvantages for the political advantages it had once seen in the process of European integration. And the European governments were no longer prepared to accept the restraints on national freedom of action that common policies in fields like energy and money would have implied.

To some extent, this decline in the importance attached to the process of European integration was a testimony to its success. The "German problem," which had been so important in the early years, no longer existed. Western Europe was prosperous. Despite its imperfections, there was a European Economic Community and no one inside or outside thought, or hoped, it would disappear.

By the seventies, the strongest reason for believing that the continuing development of a European entity was desirable rested on assumptions about the best distribution of power in an increasingly interdependent world in which U.S. power was declining relative to that of other countries. The international economic environment was changing. The two-pillar European-Atlantic relationship, which had such a strong attraction for Macmillan and many others on both sides of the Atlantic during the Kennedy administration, had given way to the more complicated five-power world view of Henry Kissinger and to the curious ambiguities that seemed to characterize the so-called Year of Europe (1973).

By the beginning of the eighties, not just in community circles but everywhere, there were few signs of what used to be called the "communitarian spirit," an attitude that not only characterized the community of six in the early days but also the OEEC in its golden period. Those who were active in those first postwar years are now old, and like all the elderly they doubtless exaggerate the joys and virtues of the past. It is harder to break new ground now than it was then. It is always easier to write on a clean slate. Perhaps—as some scholars today would argue—the Americans and the Europeans who worked so closely together in those years were at times a little naive. But they were not afraid to be bold. And the mixture paid off. It was a uniquely creative period.

7

The Implications
of the Marshall Plan

DAVID CALLEO

The Marshall Plan was not only an American initiative to reju-
venate European economies, it was also an essential step toward
forming the entire postwar global system. That system has always
depended upon a fundamental geopolitical alliance between the
United States and Western Europe. The Marshall Plan cemented
that alliance. Thanks to the Marshall Plan, Europe was able to
complete its economic and political recovery and join with the
United States in the creation of a liberal international order. This
order has greatly benefited the United States, Europe, and the
world in general.

The problem now, however, is that the world has changed so
greatly since the late 1940s. If the system built then is to be preserved, it must be adapted; the relationship between the United
States and Europe needs a fundamental readjustment.

From the beginning, there have been great tensions in that
relationship. Some of these tensions were apparent during World
War II. Along with the obvious conflict between the United States
and Germany, there were serious difficulties among the Allies.

The memoirs of Cordell Hull, for example, sometimes give the impression that World War II was between the United States and Britain. Hull was preoccupied with how to break down the protectionist block created out of the British Empire in the 1930s. A good part of Hull's memoirs reflect his concern that the British Empire should not continue as a trading block. Winston Churchill's response was that he had not become prime minister in order to preside over the liquidation of the British Empire.

Similarly, General Charles de Gaulle's memoirs suggest that World War II was between the United States and France. De Gaulle believed, not without reason, that Roosevelt was not interested in the revival of the traditional European states. Roosevelt did tend to see Europe as the place from whence most of the world's troubles arose; he was ambivalent as to whether its states should reassert themselves in their traditional world role.

Most of the tension among France, Britain, and the United States during the war had to do with the future of the European colonial empires. The United States envisioned an end to colonialism and the creation of a liberal international order with national independence for what is now called the Third World. The British envisioned a commonwealth that would grant independence to most of the British Empire while preserving strong political and economic ties, as well as something of Britain's global role as a great power. The French struggled to hang on to their empire and clung to the notion that the great European powers should remain world powers.

The British and French views conflicted head on with Roosevelt's ideas. From a European point of view, it was easy to see the American enthusiasm for independence in the Third World as simply a form of American imperialism. De Gaulle called it "the will to power cloaked in idealism." If the British and the French were ejected from their global positions around the world, the Americans would supplant them. The Americans were so powerful economically, as well as politically and militarily, that they did not need to establish formal colonial relationships. They could dominate simply because their power was so overwhelming.

Aside from these global rivalries, there later emerged rival conceptions of postwar Europe. Broadly speaking, the United States, and many Europeans, favored the notion of a supranational or federal construction. The French Gaullists and the British favored a more nationalist conception, a Europe of states that would cooperate with each other to enhance their national power. De Gaulle once observed that nations join an alliance to preserve their independence, not to give it up. European cooperation was not to diminish the power of France as a national state, but to enhance it.

As De Gaulle saw it, European institutions, including the Common Market, existed to give the European states more control over their national economic environment than they would have had if they did not cooperate with each other. Without cooperation, for instance, they would not achieve the scale necessary to compete with an enormous economic power like the United States. Until now, at least, this nationalist idea of Europe is what has prevailed.

A Europe of states, however, has certain inherent vulnerabilities. It needs a fundamental consensus to hold its independent members together. Most coalitions or alliances form in the face of a common antagonist; it is easier to form an alliance against something than on behalf of unity for its own sake.

In the case of the North Atlantic Treaty Organization (NATO), the antagonist was fairly obvious and the situation posed few intellectual ambiguities. For the Common Market, the problem was more delicate, since the obvious antagonist against which the European national economies needed to unite was the United States. This was not because of any unremitting hostility between Europe and the United States, or of any lack of common interest between them, but rather because of a need to achieve a comparable economic scale if Europeans were to coexist in an interdependent world economy with the Americans. Had the Common Market not given the European states this economic stature, the world economy might well have recreated the protectionist arrangements typical of the interwar period.

The need for consensus within a coalition of states imposes limitations on the extent of membership. The Common Market initially included six countries, drawn from Western, Central, and

Southern Europe. Excluded were all of Northern Europe and all of Eastern Europe, including the eastern half of Germany. This division was of particular concern to the Germans because if Europe was to be defined as the original six countries—or the original six bolstered by Britain, Scandinavia, and the Iberian countries—it implied the permanent division of Germany. The separation of West and East Germany was also of concern to the French, in part because they realized its potential for disrupting Germany's adherence to any essentially West European coalition. De Gaulle tried to reconcile a West European coalition with some eventual pan-European construction by way of his vision of a Europe that stretched from the Atlantic to the Urals.

By the late 1960s, the Germans appeared to be giving substance to the French fears. Instead of a tightly organized Western Europe allied with the United States, leaders like Egon Bahr began to revive a pan-European vision in which a neutral but united Germany floated between the superpowers. This was a German nationalist version of de Gaulle's idea of a united but neutral European block floating between the superpowers. The Gaullist vision also saw the Soviet empire gradually declining as the Asian states began to rise. The Soviet Union would be drawn into Europe and ultimately forced to change her regime. Pan-European visions notwithstanding, both West Germany and France have remained within an enlarged West European coalition and their own relationship has grown closer and more tightly structured.

Meanwhile, the Common Market has become by far the most interesting and successful experiment in intergovernmental cooperation in modern times. In effect, a European political economic block has been created which has made it possible for Europe to live interdependently with the United States on terms of rough equality.

In the military sphere, however, there has been a different kind of relationship, which, in many respects, amounts to an American military protectorate for Western Europe: NATO. The most enthusiastic supporters of NATO in its early days were not to be found in the U.S. State Department, but among the French and the British. There was a good deal of opposition within the U.S.

government to NATO because of fears that Europe would grow militarily dependent on the United States and that, in turn, the United States, once it had troops in Europe, would never find the political will to get them out. Furthermore, having U.S. troops permanently stationed in Europe would make the resolution of the German problem impossible and would militarize Europe in a way that was in the interest of neither the Americans nor the West Europeans.

These arguments, put forth most powerfully by George Kennan, were hotly debated within the State Department before the NATO treaty was signed. The strong U.S. opposition to NATO was based not on a rejection of the basic alliance between the United States and Europe, but on a rejection of the dominant military role that the United States would play within that alliance. There was considerable reluctance in the United States to launch a large-scale military rearmament effort. It was only with the advent of the Korean War that the political scales tipped in favor of a major military buildup.

Initially, the great supporters of NATO were not the Americans, but rather the French and the British. Both wished to proceed with their global ambitions and did not want to be responsible for maintaining large armies on the European continent. France, for example, was fighting a big colonial war in Indochina. As soon as the French disentangled themselves from that war, they became embroiled in another colonial war in Algeria, which constituted a further large-scale military effort beyond the confines of Europe. These military activities overseas made the French and the British particularly eager to have the Americans take over the defense of Europe.

In the early days of NATO, and ever since, the United States has been able to maintain its dominant military role essentially because of its lead in nuclear weapons, which has allowed the United States to maintain its European protectorate relatively cheaply. If the United States had been required to maintain a standing army large enough to balance that of the Soviet Union, the alliance would not have lasted. The economic and political strain on the United States of maintaining such a large mobilized army in Europe either would have precipitated a war with the

Soviets to finally settle the European situation or forced a reneging by the United States on its European commitment.

NATO has been a good deal for the Europeans. Not only has it provided comfortable security without requiring a heavy military input, but its political-diplomatic price has been low. The alliance has not, for example, prevented Europeans from pursuing with the Soviets whatever is to be gained by diplomatic, political, or economic initiatives in the East. The limits to their success cannot reasonably be blamed on NATO. That Germany, or Europe, is not reunited cannot be laid to the Atlantic Alliance, even if it is a convenient scapegoat for these failures. The real problem rests in the unwillingness or inability of the Soviets, because of their backward and repressive political economy, to accept more intimate economic or political relations with the West.

In the Third World, the old rivalry between the United States and Western Europe over global influence has created some difficult moments. One such moment was the Suez crisis in 1956, when the British and French tried to reassert their old colonial role in a particularly forceful fashion and found no support from the United States. In many ways, the oil crises have also had much to do with the U.S.-European rivalry in the Middle East and elsewhere in the Third World.

Though this rivalry has continued since World War II, on the whole the Pax Americana has guaranteed European interests. It has given Europeans access to raw materials, including oil, at reasonable prices. Furthermore, Europeans have discovered that they are able to sustain much of their global influence in this postwar system, sometimes rather economically.

This postwar system, however, is now in serious difficulty. The root of the problem is that the system has been "hegemonic" and has depended heavily on the economic power of the United States. This economic power has now declined rather sharply from its great preponderance in the 1950s. The decline is, of course, relative. In absolute terms, the United States has more modern weapons and is richer and more populous than in 1945, but in relative terms the United States has lost ground to the rest of the world. A simple statistic can serve to illustrate this point: Whereas the United States produced roughly one-half of the world's industrial goods in 1950, it now produces roughly one-quarter.

This relative decline of U.S. power is not a sign of U.S. failure. On the contrary, it is a sign of the fulfillment of the U.S. postwar policy that encouraged the reconstruction of Western Europe and Japan. Western Europe and Japan are now thoroughly rejuvenated, with the result that they are economically (and, in the case of Western Europe, even militarily) much stronger in relation to the United States than they were in 1945 or 1950.

Similarly, the aim of U.S. policy has never been to destroy the Soviet Union, but rather to contain it, a policy that has forced the Soviets to live in peace for over forty years. The Soviet Union is much stronger now, in many respects, than it was at the end of World War II, when it was a relatively underdeveloped country.

Above all, it has been U.S. policy in the postwar era to stimulate development in the Third World. This has resulted in increasingly severe industrial competition, not to mention increased military challenges. In short, this change in the relative position of the United States vis-à-vis the rest of the world is not a sign of U.S. failure; it is the natural consequence of the policies that the United States has purposefully followed.

This change does create a problem, however, for a world system whose institutions have been so hegemonic, so heavily dependent on an overwhelming U.S. predominance. The United States no longer has the resources to fulfill that same leading role. In attempting to go on with the role without the proper resources, it has indulged in economic practices that are self-defeating in the long run not only for the U.S. economy, but also for the world economy. This raises the unhappy possibility that the United States has become a "hegemon in decline."

Hegemony implies that there is one power that has a special management role. Exploitation of this relationship is a complicated question. In many ways, it is the hegemon who is exploited and the others are "free riders." When, over a period of several decades, others get a free ride on the public goods provided by the hegemon (like military security), the hegemon can become overextended and begin to decline. A hegemon in decline becomes a power that, instead of supporting the system, begins to manipulate the system to support itself. If the prolonged manipulation begins to break the system down, the whole hegemonic relationship becomes self-defeating.

This theory is an embarrassingly useful tool for interpreting U.S. monetary behavior in the last two decades. The pendulum-like nature of U.S. monetary policy is not the result of some inherent wickedness or stupidity in U.S. policy, although some of each may exist in the policy of any country. Rather, the behavior developed when the United States was forced to bear burdens for which it lacked the necessary resources.

This relative decline could have in it the makings of a great historical tragedy; now that the United States is not able to continue in its hegemonic role, the whole postwar global system could collapse. On the other hand, the U.S. decline could be offset by a more pluralistic form of global management, a topic that points back to U.S.-European relations. NATO in particular and the U.S.-European relationship in general form a microcosm that replicates what has happened in the world. The NATO alliance continues to rely heavily on the U.S. military contribution, even though the military and economic rationale for U.S. dominance within NATO has all but disappeared. The nature of this problem, the overburdening of the U.S. position in NATO, suggests its own solution—a larger European role within the alliance. This must not mean the end of U.S. participation in the alliance, but rather a shift of the primary leadership and responsibility for running the alliance to the Europeans. The United States should be the ally and guarantor of Western Europe, but not its hegemonic defense manager and protector. It is particularly important that France and Britain take their proper roles in Western European defense. The United States must stop providing each with its traditional pretext for limited engagement.

There is a parallel between what is needed now in the military sphere and what happened with the Marshall Plan in the economic sphere. By the late 1940s, it was understood that Europe needed some form of economic integration of its own if it was to remain and flourish within a liberal Atlantic economy. The Marshall Plan helped encourage this European integration, as the necessary condition for a stable transatlantic and global economy. The Europeans, encouraged by the Americans, continued down the path to the Common Market.

The difference between then and now is that the will to change has waned since World War II. At the end of that war, heroism did not seem out of place as people vividly recalled what happened when countries failed to deal with the problems of the international system *before* those problems had deteriorated beyond control. More than forty years of peace and comfort have blunted any lingering enthusiasm for heroic initiatives.

Within the U.S. government, there is great reluctance to give up the leadership of Europe held since World War II. Although successive administrations complain a great deal that the Europeans do not bear enough of the burden of common defense, each seeks to continue to run European defense and none, therefore, is willing to do anything serious to shift its burdens. Many U.S. officials also find it difficult even to imagine a relationship with Europe that is not hegemonic. As the strategic and economic burden has grown increasingly insupportable, a curious symbiotic relationship has developed between those who want to hang on to the traditional hegemonic relationship until the last possible moment and those who want to disengage entirely. These two perspectives reinforce each other. Together they crowd out of the public imagination any notion of a "devolution" that would pass the basic defense responsibility and leadership to the Europeans while permitting the United States to continue making a vital contribution to the alliance.

The Europeans have similar problems with their political imaginations. There is, above all, the West German question. For the West Germans, forming a close military partnership with France means writing off the popular dream of a neutral West Germany floating protected within a military balance sustained by the superpowers. Should the military balance in Europe be maintained primarily by the Europeans, West Germany would have to discipline its dreams in order to help maintain the European military balance. While this is precisely what the West Germans have been doing for several decades, a certain part of their collective political imagination has cherished the vision of reunification through neutralism and disengagement—an escapist fantasy from the harsh lessons of German history. It is particularly difficult at this point for the West Germans to give up that fantasy because, for the first time in the postwar period, a Soviet government has come along that knows how to nourish and indulge it.

Meanwhile, the French, increasingly worried about the West Germans, cling to the present tottering regime, both because it has long given them a degree of security never before experienced and because they still fear that any serious initiative will antagonize Americans and Europeans alike.

As the present system grows increasingly unworkable, it remains difficult to overcome the widespread diffidence toward changing it. Perhaps, as we celebrate the burst of European and U.S. creativity which accompanied the development of the Marshall Plan, we should also note that the great accomplishments of that era are in danger. Maybe we should ask ourselves whether our own leadership is not being put to a similar test.

8

A Second
Marshall Plan

WASSILY LEONTIEF

The immediate economic aim of the Marshall Plan was to reconstruct Europe, one of the most productive areas of the world, after the devastation of World War II. One well-defined objective of the plan was to rebuild structures on the foundations that remained. But reconstruction was not limited to the physical process. Science and technology had also been adversely affected by the war. The Marshall Plan required participating countries to accumulate counterfunds in their own currency to support students, intellectuals, professors, and science. This investment in human resources enabled participating countries to reconstruct themselves intellectually, scientifically, and professionally as well as physically. Soviet leaders, however, refused to take part in the Marshall Plan. They did not want to jeopardize fundamental objectives and policies in order to receive economic assistance.

Russia had been an industrial empire before the Russian Revolution. In 1800, it produced more steel for military purposes than did England. Production fell back in the nineteenth century and

Russia developed slowly, even though it was maintaining a large army and building a trans-Siberian railroad. The Industrial Revolution that transformed Western Europe and the United States left the Russians behind. Currently, the United States is the largest economic power in the world, although its dominant role diminishes as the rest of the world develops. The Soviet Union is the second largest in terms of its internal economic situation, but in terms of international trade figures it plays a small role in the world economy.

One cannot discuss the relationship between the United States and the Soviet Union without attending to the changes being made under Mikhail Gorbachev's leadership. Recent developments in the Soviet Union may have a strong, long-term impact on the world; from a Soviet point of view, these developments are nearly as important as the Russian Revolution. Gorbachev's decision to effect change must be interpreted in light of a cognizance of history on the part of the Soviet leadership. Gorbachev makes his decisions for domestic reasons, not for purposes of foreign policy. He recognizes that unless change occurs, the Soviet Union will slowly regress.

The Russian economy has been improving by about 1 percent a year, but there is a great deal of discontent in the country. Running an economy can easily be likened to sailing a ship. One needs wind in order to move and a rudder in order to steer. Russian leaders recognize that the propelling force needed in all "free countries" is self-interest. The profit motive is the wind that has propelled the Western economies and that now propels formerly less developed countries like Japan, Korea, and Taiwan. These latter countries have clearly demonstrated how the individual pursuit of profits promotes economic development and the introduction of new technology.

Russia had a big rudder, but it lowered the sails. Without wind the rudder will not move and cannot direct a ship. Likewise, economic policies are not effective if there is nothing to propel the country forward. Gorbachev recognizes this dilemma. He does not want to reproduce the American society and economy, but he does want to take advantage of the motivation that profit seeking generates. Introducing a quasi-capitalist society in a

Socialist country may be as difficult as introducing socialism in a capitalist society.

In a tradition that goes back to the old czarist regimes, writers, journalists, scientists, and engineers have always played a great role in Russian politics. In the United States, intellectuals do not play the same role as do business people. Gorbachev understands that he has to gain the support of the intellectuals. He has called them the yeast of society, saying that without this yeast the bread will not rise. He knows that intellectuals consider freedom of expression vital to their lives and to their work, and so he has introduced *glasnost:* limited freedom of discussion, limited freedom of the press, and less censorship.

It is easier to introduce limited freedom of the press than to reconstruct an entire economic system. Not only are people more accustomed to following bureaucratic directions than to exercising private initiative, but they are also working within a structure that was not built for free enterprise. Profit-generating activities require a different infrastructure. For example, small farmers living 2,000 miles from Moscow will be hard pressed to sell their produce in a market when they have little or no access to railroads or highways. Further compounding the difficulty of effecting change is the tendency of transitions to cause a system to lose efficiency. The Soviet's next concern should be whether their general population will support reform if their economic situation does not improve, or even deteriorates, in the next couple of years. Intellectuals make up a minority of the population; most people are not as interested in freedom of the press as in how much bread and butter is available.

The problem, from our point of view, is that we observe the Soviet Union as if we were watching a play; we alternately applaud and criticize. Perhaps we do not recognize the importance of the outcome of the play. Success or failure by Gorbachev will have a strong impact on the economic and political world. Some people would like him to fail because they assume that if the Soviet Union is weak, the Western side of the arms race will have some advantage. In fact, however, a weak Soviet Union would build up a larger army than would a strong Soviet Union. If Gorbachev fails, the danger of military conflict will be great. If he wins, the Soviet Union will be economically stronger and will be able to participate in the world economy on a larger scale. The economic, social, and political antagonism between East and West would thus be reduced. So it is important to the West that Gorbachev succeed. How might we be able to help? Economic assistance to maintain the standard of living, for example, might be of critical importance if Soviet reconstruction is to produce results.

Relationships among the West, East, North, and South have been complicated for several hundred years. Since the Industrial Revolution, in which first Europe and later the United States made incredible progress, there has been an explosion in population growth, economic development, and per capita income growth in those areas. Other parts of the world have slowly begun to develop too, but the pace has been extremely uneven. The pattern is much like that of a caravan of camels crossing a desert. It is a long, long road. The front camels are strong. They are proceeding nicely and approaching an oasis. The back camels are weak. Many of them cannot keep up and they fall by the roadside and die. And this journey lasts a long time.

The difference is that, in the beginning, we did not notice how bad social and economic conditions were in less-developed countries. With the development of modern technology, trade and communications have made us conscious of the disparities; communication between the front and back of the caravan has become intense. Transportation technology makes it possible to develop local and international trade to an extent previously unthinkable. Communication systems make large populations conscious of what happens in other countries. A world economic system exists on the basis of great interdependence among countries, and this interdependence creates reasons both for cooperation and for conflict.

In the early 1970s, the Dutch government funded a United Nations effort to project the future development of the world economy from 1970 to 2000. Because so much is unknown in such a projection of the future, the analysts made alternative assumptions and developed two extreme projections, one positing the old economic order and the other positing a new economic order.

The basic assumption of the old economic order projection was

that, in the future as in the past, the less-developed countries
would have to maintain balanced trade. They would not receive
aid and would have to pay for imports by exporting goods in a
completely balanced system. The new economic order projection
was based on an entirely different assumption. The assumption
was that measures could be taken to freeze or decrease the gap
in the standard of living between developed and less-developed
countries. The most obvious measure to accomplish that goal was
for developed countries to import more than they export. In other
words, less-developed countries would have to receive a great
deal of capital.

From 1970 to 1980, less-developed countries grew faster than
the optimistic projections predicted. Those countries that fared
the best did not simply sell their natural resources, like oil,
but began to develop by increasing their productive capacities.
They were able to make these gains because of the Organization
of Petroleum Exporting Countries (OPEC). OPEC extracted a ter-
rific amount of money from the United States and Europe. It then
lent that money back to the Western banks. The Western banks
could not invest it all in the United States and Europe, and so
they lent it to less-developed countries at high interest rates, or-
ganizing a private, improvised Marshall Plan for developing
countries. Despite the absence of elegance in that plan, it enabled
many less-developed countries to advance. Progress was insuf-
ficient, but efficiency cannot be expected of less-developed countries.

The system grew quickly and then suddenly stopped. Large
Western banks faced bankruptcies. The indebtedness is not yet
solved and there is still debate about how to handle the situation.
The United States cannot afford for established banks to go bankrupt; it indirectly prevents those banks from folding by giving
money to the less-developed countries, thus preventing them
from going bankrupt and enabling them to pay their debts. There
is a certain advantage to this system in that it permits less-
developed countries to continue to develop at the rate maintained
from 1970 to 1980.

In 1984, the head of a Brazilian central bank resigned. He said
he could not remain president of a bank if Brazil accepted the

as the board of governors of the Federal Reserve System and Harvard University. People were attracted to the comparative independence of this new Economic Cooperation Administration as well as to its hiring procedures and salary scales.

It would be a mistake to think that the Marshall Plan was the first massive postwar U.S. aid program. By the time the Marshall Plan began, the United States had already expended almost $17 billion abroad in grants and loans. The plan itself was originally expected to cost $17 billion over a period of four and one-quarter years. In other words, the scope of the Marshall Plan, the magnitude in financial terms, was about the same as the combined scope of the United Nations Relief and Rehabilitation Administration, aid to refugees, aid to Japan, aid to Germany, aid to China, and a variety of other aid programs, including a large U.S. stabilization loan to Britain in 1946.

Although the Marshall Plan was not the beginning of U.S. aid, it was the first U.S. aid that followed a plan. Its projected duration—four years and three months—was uneven because the plan was so urgent that it started right away instead of at the beginning of the next fiscal year. It also treated Western Europe as a unit. It was called the European Recovery Program—not the Recovery Program for Iceland, Greece, Italy, Belgium, or Luxembourg. Previous U.S. aid had always been purely bilateral. For example, military aid to China had nothing to do with other countries in the Far East. Support to Germany and Japan was essentially uncoordinated with any other nations.

To enhance the notion that Europe was indeed the political structure that was both to receive the aid and to perform some collective administrative functions, the United States required that Europeans get together and submit a statement of Europe's economic needs. Thus, the Committee for European Economic Cooperation (CEEC) was established and operating in Paris not long after General Marshall made his June 1947 speech at Harvard. The key word in the CEEC title was cooperation. There was a strong underlying belief not only that Europe needed to operate as a unit in order to make an efficient recovery from the war, but also that there should be a goal of some form of political integration. The CEEC, later converted to the Organization for European

Economic Cooperation (OEEC), was to be part of the infrastructure for various kinds of political integration.

And some integration did result. A coal and steel community developed as a direct result of the Marshall Plan. There was never a full-scale European Defense Community (EDC), but a European Payments Union was established. Although interest in the political integration of Europe remained strong among the U.S. officials dealing with the Marshall Plan in Washington, D.C., it dissolved among those who worked in the central European offices. Political integration was not taken seriously in embassy missions either, except in France. In the Office of the U.S. Special Representative in Europe located in Paris, U.S. officials were dealing with genuine economic difficulties that appeared surmountable only if there were various kinds of economic integration. Political integration was a luxury for which they had no time.

There was also a contrast between U.S. officials in Europe and in Washington as to the way they administered the Marshall Plan. This plan was the first genuine experiment in international intimacy among the United States and various allied, friendly countries; the close relationship among people who worked together was unprecedented. People from sixteen nations sat around a table in Paris addressing each other by first names and candidly examining the policies of each other's countries. Because of the way the aid was administered, it became legitimate, for example, to require the French Treasury to justify its fiscal policies to somebody from the Central Bank of Belgium. This kind of unclothing, of revelation, of reciprocal examination, had probably never occurred before.

Working together on common projects and on each other's recovery programs proved to be critical processes for the establishment of NATO as well. People had to familiarize themselves with routines, procedures, each other, and what the governments of some countries could and could not acknowledge. They had to read, write, and talk about each country's domestic and international economic policies. They had to learn what was best done in cloakrooms and what was best done in meeting rooms.

The United States tried to get the European countries to make most of the decisions. They usually succeeded in getting European participation, but they rarely managed to assign the whole job to the Europeans. One of the first questions to arise was whether Marshall aid was to be given strictly to governments or to other recipients as well. It was ultimately decided that since reconstruction goals, such as dredging a canal or building a factory, would require the use of indigenous resources, the aid should be administered government to government.

Aid was meant to be used to buy import commodities from places in which payment had to be in dollars, such as the United States, the Western Hemisphere, and a few other convertible currency sources. The dollars were made available to the European governments. The European governments then sold the dollars to licensed importers, just as it would sell them dollars from export earnings. The importers paid for the dollars in French francs, or in British pounds, or in whatever the local currency was. That local currency went into an account that was owned by the government, because the government had received most of the money as an outright gift from the United States. So governments sold the gift money and kept the proceeds. The importers then imported through the usual channels and sold to their usual customers, who paid in the local currency, and the cycle started again.

The words "recovery" and "reconstruction" might suggest that most of the aid came in the form of machinery and equipment, but fewer than 10 percent of the imports financed under the Marshall Plan were capital goods. In fact, 50 percent of all the imports were food, feed stuffs, fuel, and fertilizer. The other 50 percent included iron, steel, aluminum, copper, and zinc. Local labor was used to build dredges and to dig canals. Electric power was needed in the dredge factories, and that was produced by coal or oil bought through the Marshall Plan. Steel and metal-working machinery may have been bought through the Marshall Plan as well. Most factories, houses, roads, railroads, canals, and airfields were built using imported materials. It came as a surprise to members of Congress that little machinery or equipment was financed. They had envisioned exporting a great deal of both. It did not occur to them that Europe might need coal and oil to make the most of its recovery.

The planners hoped that, within four years, the Europeans would be able to pay for all the imports they needed from the dollar area, either through conversion or by producing these goods themselves and thus building up their export potential. The planners thought that, over a period of four years, a balance of payments could be reached. Closure of the Marshall Plan could be measured, not by counting completed projects or by measuring local standards of living, but rather by finding that most of the governments were capable of managing their own foreign trade without having a balance of payments deficit. In those days, some people believed that the United States would have a chronic balance of payments surplus for the rest of the century.

In the first year, the Marshall Plan contributed $5.5 billion. There was never an explicit principle dictating the division of aid among countries, although the planners understood that every country ought to get some aid. It was clear that the plan was not an equalization program. There was no intention to target the aid to those areas in which it would most increase levels of income and production, nor even to increase, for example, the Italian standard of living up to that of the British. Neither did the plan intend to exclude countries that seemed poor candidates for economic growth.

A precedent was established early on to identify crucial imports that countries could not afford. A great deal of scrutiny went into which imports countries could get along without and which they were justified in having. Although it was rarely put in such terms, decisions were made about the proper diet for the British and the appropriate degree of gasoline rationing in France or Germany. It was as though economic experts, like family doctors, wrote out prescriptions for what countries absolutely needed under the assumption that belts could be tightened a bit and countries that were used to less comfort would get along with less comfort.

The United States was unable to get the OEEC countries to make the painful decisions as to what their own aid shares should be. These decisions were somewhat competitive; once the appropriation was made and the funds were fixed, a country that appealed for a larger share knew that an adjustment would come at the expense of another country. If, for example, Italy wanted a larger share, it would have to claim, in the presence of representatives from other countries, that it deserved more of the aid. That understanding protected the United States against coercive importuning.

The next question was whether the aid amounts should be fixed or flexible. One possibility was to guarantee reimbursement after the fact: Countries could run up deficits that the United States would pay at the end of the year. But the fear was that too much flexibility might encourage countries to aggravate their own needs. Such aggravation would not necessarily be fraudulent, but every country would think its own needs had been underestimated and underappreciated by the granting agency. Leaders would therefore believe that they had a justifiable case if they ran out of funds before the end of year and needed more.

Another alternative was to give a set amount of aid. If the country received more than it needed, it could save it. If there was not enough, the country would have to manage as best it could. The latter possibility had important incentive effects; countries would not be tempted to overspend and then ask for extra help. The U.S. Office of Management and Budgets uses this same technique at the present time: It apportions funds to agencies over the year to keep agencies from spending their budget disproportionately early in the year and thus coming up short at the end.

The dilemma was never resolved: Was it best to fix aid amounts for incentive effects, or to keep them flexible because of incentive effects, or to keep them flexible because of uncertainties about what countries would need? One year the United States announced that neither would it make up shortfalls at the end of the year, nor would it withhold funds from countries that could get along by spending less than was projected. This announcement was dubious, since it was clear that the United States would grant an amount in the second half of the year which was consistent with what it had granted in the first half. The claim that an amount was fixed in advance did not seem plausible.

The choice of which imports were to require payments by the

nations became a strategic issue. All recipient countries had some dollars of their own to spend. Greece must have been able to afford only one-quarter of its imports, but Britain could pay for more than one-half. Although, in theory, it would seem wise to restrict financing to hard-core essentials, doing so would mean the financing of what another country would have had to import and pay for in any case. To influence what another country imports, goods must be purchased which can substitute for what it might otherwise buy, such as various kinds of equipment or pharmaceuticals. But if Congress were to determine nonessential goods were being financed, it could object. For example, nylon had been shipped to Europe under the Marshall Plan; members of Congress thought that it was being used for hosiery. They did not deem stockings to be part of European recovery, and so the Europeans were allowed to spend their own money on nylon while the United States procured for them other goods that pertained more to the U.S. image of recovery and reconstruction.

European governments often secretly wanted the United States to control the use of their aid. Governments were subject to pressures from farmers, industrialists, importers, and consumers. Often, when a European government had to deny import licenses for goods from the dollar area, it made the excuse that the United States would not pay for that purchase. Consequently, the U.S. government became a useful scapegoat.

A similar manipulation of economic and government relations involved counterpart funds. Each government put the local currency funds that it obtained by selling Marshall Plan dollars into a central bank. Except for a few legal restrictions in some governments, creating accounts in the name of the government at the central bank was quite easy. The accounts could be opened or closed so easily that one might have thought counterpart funds were paper transactions of no economic significance. In fact, many parliamentarians in Britain and elsewhere acted as though these accounts, which had to be openly published, held free money. Even though the British government may have thought that it would be inflationary, given its budget, to spend either counterpart funds or money borrowed from the Central Bank, many back-benchers in the Labor Party wanted to spend those funds.

They exerted a great deal of pressure both on the Bank of England and on the British Treasury.

To reduce some of this pressure, the United States wanted to close the account by paying off a short-term debt at the Bank of England. Congress, however, did not want it to look as if a Socialist government that had nationalized many of its industries was to have its debts paid by the U.S. aid program. To ensure that the accounts disappeared and that the Labor members of Parliament did not get their hands on the funds, the Economic Cooperation Administration had to construct an acceptable way for the British to pay off their national debt. Counterpart accounts were often used as an excuse to legitimize the U.S. government's examination of other countries' fiscal and monetary policies, as well as to encourage similar examinations among European countries.

Some aid was made conditional on the establishment of drawing rights. All Belgian counterpart funds had to be put at the disposal of other European countries for use in procuring imports from Belgium. Proud of its fiscal and monetary stability, Belgium was able to scrutinize, examine, and interrogate the recipients of drawing rights because it was being asked by the United States to put up its own currency for the use of France, Italy, or Britain. Because Belgium, in effect, became an aid-giving nation, it was therefore in a position, along with the United States, to be able to examine publicly the domestic fiscal policies of other recipient countries.

In 1952, the Korean War caused the direction of the Marshall Plan to change. For most of the next year, the United States tried to convert the European Recovery Program into a program for European military buildup, changing its name to the Mutual Security Program. The military equipment portion of the program was used to finance dollar imports and was labeled as defense support. Despite these nominal changes, the underlying economic transition was so smooth that it was hardly a transition at all. The shift in emphasis from reconstruction to defense did not necessitate a change in imports. Countries needed food, feed stuffs, fuel, and fertilizer to train an army, just as they did to dredge a canal. Military equipment had already been provided to

European countries alongside the Marshall Plan. Ultimately, the bulk of the military buildup was accomplished by increasing the number of military personnel. This increase was largely financed by the currency of the individual countries and so had little impact upon the need for imports.

The U.S. military services wanted to send Europe military items that had been produced in the United States. In so doing, they could replace their old equipment. But the Europeans had the capacity to produce a great deal of what they needed at home. At the beginning of the buildup, they needed such basic equipment as trucks, which they were already producing for civilians. In addition, the means of production of artillery and ammunition were crude and simple: The Europeans required proximity fuses from the United States, but they could produce the expensive parts themselves. Luckily for Europe, Congress did not turn military equipment aid over to the Defense Department, but left it in the hands of the director of Mutual Security, Averell Harriman. Harriman determined that the military services should procure military equipment for the Europeans *in* Europe. The United States even went so far as to procure guns and ammunition for the French military forces in France, thereby generating a huge boost in French exports, as the equipment was sold to the United States in return for dollars.

Indeed, the sole motivation behind the Offshore Procurement (OSP) program was to provide dollars to the Europeans from military equipment appropriations. As Congress lost enthusiasm and defense support began to taper off, appropriations for military equipment were used to procure goods in Europe, which allowed these countries to export $4–5 billion worth of goods to each other, and sometimes to themselves.

Occasionally there was also financial disguise. The war raging in Indochina was much more popular in Congress than was the defense buildup in Europe. When it became difficult to give the French the dollar assistance they needed, the United States procured over $1 billion worth of munitions and supplies in France for use by French troops in Indochina. In other words, the government gave them $1.25 billion, pretending to be buying good military equipment for them.

Once the emphasis shifted to defense support and commitments were made to some kind of NATO buildup, the U.S. government once again tried to get the Europeans to work out what shares they should get by conducting a burden-sharing exercise. Burden sharing was not much different from sharing aid. Aid sharing focused on what a country needed, which was always dependent on internal needs. Burden sharing focused on what a country was doing, which was always reflected in its import needs. Negotiations changed from merely haggling over what imports were needed to haggling over what defense goals should be set and what penalties would apply if the goals were not reached.

In the spring of 1952, the Temporary Council Committee (TCC) sat in Paris. It was made up of three of the same people, going through the same motions, with the same staffs and routines, as in the purer days of the Marshall Plan. By choosing France as the site of these headquarters, NATO was put in the same city as the OEEC and the overseas office of the United States Aid Administration. This placement advertised the end of the Marshall Plan and of recovery-based aid and the initiation of a new kind of aid—defense support—which was exclusively oriented toward the NATO buildup. It was as if somebody had renamed a baseball team. It was still the same game, the same players, and the franchise was still in the same city, but the names were changed from Marshall Plan and European Recovery to NATO and defense support. The Marshall Plan had not only made an essential contribution to European recovery, but it had also created a team that knew how to play the game.

10

Issues of Defense and the Atlantic Alliance

PHILIP WINDSOR

The North Atlantic Treaty Organization (NATO) is generally referred to as an alliance, but it is in fact a peculiar institution quite unlike traditional alliances. The NATO states communicate intimately in many areas and coordinate their policies to a greater degree than any other alliance in history. Yet they are not pledged to go to war on behalf of each other. The NATO treaty has no *casus foederis* and neither does it have a *casus belli*—even in spite of the famous Article Five, which declares that an attack upon one member will be regarded as an attack upon all. Yet one may search Article Five in vain for any pledge to go to war. All the same, it is assumed that if any NATO state were attacked the others would come to its aid by military means. Why?

The answer is twofold. It lies in part in the preamble to the NATO treaty, which speaks of shared and common values. That is historically most unusual: Alliances in the past have been matters of convenience and were frequently drawn up between states that had very little time for each other's values. Here, one might simply reflect that a commitment to values is always stronger than a commitment to interests. This provokes the second consideration. It is understood that the NATO members will go to war to defend each other because of the U.S. strategic guarantee—which has been in operation since at least 1954, when the United States threatened the Soviet Union with strategic retaliation should it attack U.S. allies. But while the common values persist, that U.S. strategic guarantee has come into question. I shall argue here that, although it is frequently taken for granted that the alliance and the guarantee come down to the same thing, the survival of the Atlantic Alliance may now depend upon the erosion of the strategic guarantee.

That argument can only make sense if it is presented in a historical context. Part of the peculiarity of NATO lies in the fact that, in its beginnings, it was not so much an alliance as an alternative system for the conduct of international affairs. This system arose when it became clear that the wartime cooperation between the United States and the Soviet Union would not last. Roosevelt had expected the postwar world to be fashioned by a Soviet-U.S. understanding. When such hopes were dashed, the United States, Britain, and more gradually the other European powers turned toward a different enterprise: an international system based on Western cooperation. Perhaps the turning point lay in Stalin's rejection of the Marshall Plan. It was that rejection that, above all, provided the impetus for transatlantic cooperation among the Western powers and the U.S. underwriting of European recovery. In the face of enduring Soviet hostility, NATO was the logical consequence of the process begun by the Marshall Plan.

Moreover, the NATO model became the basis of a kind of global organization. In the period immediately following the formation of NATO, for example, the United States pressured Britain to form a Middle East Defense Organization. The plan fell apart when Egypt refused to join, but a revised version led to the Baghdad Pact and, subsequently, the Central Treaty Organization (CENTO). Similarly, Britain and France, alongside the United States, were members of the Southeast Asian Treaty Organization (SEATO). But those alliances have now disappeared. NATO has endured, but the early framework that was provided for purposes of international cooperation is now, as its limitations become increasingly apparent, receding in favor of a different pattern: the pattern of the classical alliance. The intimacy and the American commitment remain strong. That commitment is manifested in hundreds of ways, not limited to the workings of the NATO bureaucracy. Yet it is still true to say that the NATO bureaucratic framework helps to shelter governments and to normalize relationships so that all can still make decisions based on consensus. Matters have, however, become more differentiated: The question of where NATO works and where it does not work has become increasingly important.

Certain classic disputes that have, in the past, been repeatedly resolved are now growing in saliency; the process of their resolution has been subject to ever more intense conflicts each time round. This reflects the fact that the context is changing. NATO is no longer the basis for an international order founded on Western cooperation, but rather a subordinate system within a new emerging international order. Soviet-U.S. cooperation may provide the basis for a different global understanding, no longer based exclusively on the expectations of confrontation;—if so, that would be a major factor in international relations and in European perspectives on NATO in the coming years.

The new superpower bilateralism, girded about with mutual suspicion as it is, is part of a different international order from the one in which NATO grew and functioned for so many years. Yet NATO will probably survive—especially if the strategic guarantee is no longer regarded as its key element. The shared values referred to in the preamble to the NATO treaty will do much to ensure that this is so. But they are also reflected in the conduct of American policy. At the Reykjavik summit, it appeared to many Europeans that superpower bilateralism was threatening to bypass NATO. Instead, in subsequent negotiations, the United States has carefully consulted its allies, updating them on progress, seeking their views, and heeding their anxieties. So, although the international order has changed, NATO still remains at the center of American foreign policymaking.

All the same, another aspect of the new order is the growing, if familiar, tensions between the United States and Europe. In this respect, there is a frequently voiced concern: namely, that the Soviet Union might be trying to separate the United States from Western Europe by engaging in two different policies of detente, one at the superpower level and one at the European level. In such circumstances, the Atlantic Alliance could lose its saliency in the politics of the European powers, just as superpower bilateralism could challenge the centrality of the alliance in the politics of the United States. There have been many occasions in which the West Europeans have expressed an uneasiness about superpower bilateralism. But this uneasiness only parallels the early concerns voiced by the Reagan administration over the European search for continuing detente at a time when the United States was concentrating on the global containment of the Soviet Union. In that sense, old debates within NATO have taken on new meaning as the global context changes.

That is not all. The changing nature of the global context and of East-West relations (in itself a matter for dispute between the two major areas of the Atlantic Alliance) also raises questions about the nature of NATO strategy. Relatively high levels of confrontation in Europe are still geared to a high level of nuclear risk should the unthinkable happen and war break out. The problem here is that the unthinkable is not likely to happen as the result of a sudden decision by a huddle of Soviet military, political, or KGB leaders to attack Western Europe. It is much more likely to occur as a result of interacting crises in global relationships which might feed upon each other. In 1980, for example, Helmut Schmidt, at that time the West German chancellor, remarked of the crisis in Afghanistan, of the developments which were then gathering speed in Poland, and of the crisis over the U.S. embassy hostages in Iran: "It all reminds me of 1914." He did not say 1939, which marked the deliberate aggressive intent of a single country trying to take on a continent—as was the case with the Third Reich. The war of 1914 spread by virtue of the sudden escalation and interaction of crises that had been kept under control for many years. So, while war is neither inevitable nor, as far as one can judge, even now likely, the possibility will always remain that unforeseen crises will gather speed, interact, and go out of control. In that case, should rapid nuclear escalation still be the principal means of ensuring the defense of Western Europe? In the context of different European and U.S. approaches to the changing nature of East-West relations, it might be the case that a strategy of escalation, based on the U.S. commitment, will prove the most divisive issue in alliance politics.

Yet the picture is changing. On all sides, it now appears that there is a higher interest in conventional defenses than heretofore. The potential for a longer period of conventional defense usage in the event of hostilities is already growing—thanks to the decisions taken by NATO in 1977–78 which culminated in the long-term defense program. But a changing defense posture will also need to be supplemented by measures of arms control if the alliance is to hold together.

The whole history of intermediate nuclear forces (INF) provides a case in point. At first, new intermediate-range U.S. missiles were requested by Europeans (particularly Germans) in order to "recouple" the United States to Europe, that is, to modernize the U.S. strategic guarantee. Subsequently, the deployment of INF weapons became a test case for alliance solidarity, as the United States, having acquiesced to the original European demands, observed with dismay that important political and popular movements in certain European countries were fundamentally opposed to the whole argument. At that stage, European governments had to stand up to their own public opinion in order to demonstrate their commitment to the alliance. Later still, the East-West focus on the "double-zero option" as a negotiating goal became a means of reemphasizing the importance of conventional defenses. (One might remark in passing that the INF agreement was not really a measure of arms control; it was more like a confidence-building measure. Access to verification and the exchange of information were more important than removing a small proportion of missiles. But it was widely interpreted as a significant breakthrough in the arms control process.)

Yet the agreement also emphasized certain features of alliance relations which are usually convenient to ignore. Much of my prior discussion has been couched in terms of "Europeans" versus "Americans." Yet Europeans themselves have widely different perspectives. The consequences of the INF agreement for West Germany provided a case in point: The West German dilemma might be summed up by saying that it wishes to keep as many nuclear weapons as possible and to get rid of them all as soon as possible. It wishes both to maintain a high defensive capability and to negotiate a rapid reduction of forces on the continent of Europe. On the other hand, Britain and France, as well as the United States, would like to see nuclear weapons maintained in Germany for a long time to come and to see them rapidly modernized. This is one example of how the implementation of the U.S. strategic guarantee within a changing framework of East-West security might lead to greater political disagreements within the alliance. The principle of the U.S. guarantee is still there, but the relationship between this principle and ongoing practicalities is likely to grow more irksome in the future.

Such a tendency is likely to be reinforced as the Single European Act is implemented. It is more than possible that the act will increase the pressure for European integration while also emphasizing the political disagreements among Europeans, as well as between Europeans and Americans, over the strategic goals and tactical policies that should be adopted in dealing with East-West relations.

It is in this context that some of the more traditional debates and disputes within NATO will need to be reassessed—particularly those over burden sharing. ''Burden sharing'' is really a meaningless phrase, since no one agrees on what is or should be the relationship between the European enterprise and NATO, or on the relationship between East and West. In consequence, nobody can agree on the nature of the burden prior to discussing how it should be shared. Disputes over burden sharing are, moreover, full of creative accounting—on all sides. Since civil servants and politicians in most NATO countries are sufficiently intelligent to spot each other's creative accounting, their views of each other's behavior have, along with the dispute over burden sharing itself, become increasingly acrimonious. Indeed, the whole question of burden sharing has become the symbol of a growing and differentiated ethnocentrism. U.S. strategic doctrine has, to some extent, always been formulated in an ethnocentric context and then dumped on everybody else. But today it goes further than that. In the case of all the principal NATO powers, policy is increasingly formulated and debated at home. But in the case of the Europeans, any attempt by individual countries to break out of their ethnocentric framework depends on the ability to create wider European forms of collaboration—not only in terms of defense procurement, but also in terms of closer cooperation on strategic policy. This applies even to France. In fact, on second thought, it might apply above all to France. But if European discord over arms control, and over the changing pattern of priorities in East-West relations, can lead to greater European strategic cooperation, then it is also likely to reinforce a perception on both sides of the Atlantic that Europeans and Americans are trying to pursue different kinds of goals within the same alliance.

Disputes over burden sharing are reinforced, in their effect on the alliance, by disputes over other matters, notably "out-of-area activities." It is an extraordinary fact, representing the peculiarity of NATO as an alliance, that while the treaty was being negotiated there was an intricate, and sometimes heated, debate among diplomats and politicians on both sides of the Atlantic as to whether NATO should have any restrictions at all. Nothing could better reflect the extraordinarily comprehensive view of the alliance by its original member states: They were asking, in effect, not "How big should we make it?" but "Should we limit it at all?" But once area limitations were established—the territory of the member states and of the north Atlantic Ocean down to the tropic of Cancer—the question of out-of-area activities became divisive in the affairs of NATO. In the past, that was because the United States was reluctant to support Europeans in colonial wars or in postcolonial adventures: examples include the Portuguese in Africa or the British and French in the Suez. More recently, however, the nature of the out-of-area disputes has been reversed. Today it is a question of whether Europeans support the United States in its global activities. There is a growing disposition in the United States,—in the press, on Capitol Hill, and among influential academic advisers to U.S. governments—to measure the validity of the U.S. commitment to Europe by testing the European commitment to U.S. policies. Again, there is a streak of ethnocentricity in all this: "If the United States patrols the waters of the Indian Ocean at its own expense and thereby ensures European access to Middle Eastern oil, who do those Europeans think they are if they dare to disagree with American policy in the Middle East?" That kind of argument was familiar in the years before the current oil glut; variants of it can be heard in many other contexts today. In fact, it is an extended version of the burden-sharing dispute, the fundamental assumption being that Europe pays nothing toward the cost of global security.

There is a certain tendency here to overlook what Europeans actually do. It was not the Americans, but rather the Belgians and the French, who defeated a Cuban-sponsored and Cuban-led invasion of Zaire from Angola. The fact that the United States today enjoys facilities for its Central Command (CENTCOM) force in Oman is due to the British insistence on repelling attacks on that country by the People's Democratic Republic of Yemen. There are many such instances. But what is perhaps more important is that very frequently Europeans simply disagree either with the goals or with the conduct of U.S. policy in certain parts of the world. The great majority of them, for example, have not agreed with U.S. policy in Central America during the years of the Reagan administration; many would regard that policy as counterproductive. That, in turn, raises another question, the nature of which might be clarified by an example.

In the aftermath of the Israeli invasion of Lebanon in 1982, the United States put considerable pressure on some of its European allies to take part in sending a multinational force to Beirut. The purpose was to provide a kind of impartial security force and to offer a conversational space in which the various Lebanese factions could sort out their differences while negotiations were under way as to the withdrawal of Israeli and Syrian forces from Lebanon. It was on this understanding that French, Italian, and British troops were dispatched to Lebanon. (The Italians, in particular, did a brilliant job in guarding the Palestinians and in enabling them to communicate with some of the Lebanese leaders.) Meanwhile, however, and without a word to anyone, the United States signed a Strategic Cooperation Agreement with Israel which nullified the impartiality of the multinational force and effectively turned its U.S. component into an observation agent for Israeli air strikes against Lebanon. It was in consequence of this that the Syrians decided to permit the Hezbollah car-bomb attacks that killed over 260 American marines and over 50 French paratroopers and, eventually, led to the withdrawal of the multinational force as a whole. It is this kind of U.S. behavior that, certainly in European eyes, makes it difficult to maintain the notion of any sustained out-of-area cooperation. In other words, the price of cooperation is consultation; while the United States has generally (but not always!) been scrupulous in consulting its European allies about the conduct of negotiations with the Soviet Union which affect the European theater, it has been notably less so in cases of out-of-area questions. So out-of-area relationships, which are in part extensions of burden-sharing disputes, have the potential to damage the inner relationships of the alliance itself.

A third question that haunts the politics of the alliance is that of how to achieve a more effective conventional defense posture. How much would it cost? Who will pay for it? That question turns in part upon the willingness of any of the alliance members to put up more money, in real terms, so as to cover the equipment costs that are becoming exponentially more expensive and are rising inexorably above inflation costs. Such increased real spending could procure what might be called deterrence at the operational level—as opposed to deterrence through strategic guarantee. The prevailing U.S. (and indeed European) view on this matter is that Europeans should do more to meet the costs of advanced technological equipment. But while that might look like another variant of the burden-sharing argument, it is really rather different. The defense budgets of all NATO members are declining in real terms, and it would make very little difference if Europeans were to pay a bit more proportionally than do Americans. What matters here is that the prospect of deterrence at the operational level, perfectly possible in theory, also raises the prospect of infinite demand in economic practice. (This, one might add in passing, is why defense economics is different from any other form of economics.) So, even a halfway adequate approximation of a credible defense posture is likely to mean not only greater intra-European cooperation of the kind already discussed, but also greater cooperation between the European and U.S. defense (and defense-related) industries. This will be considered in more detail as I proceed.

The fourth question raised involves heated debate over what is frequently called, in alliance jargon, the "two-way street." That is, whether the United States can make a greater contribution to the alliance as a whole by buying more defense equipment from the Europeans than, at present, it seems even remotely prepared to contemplate. After all, many European countries spend a great deal of their defense budgets in the purchase of U.S. equipment—which helps to enrich the U.S. defense industry and to keep down unit costs for purchasers in the U.S. armed services. But, by the same token, Europeans, even if they do collaborate successfully, find that unit equipment costs are high due to their limited access to the U.S. market. There are many reasons for this. In many cases, U.S. equipment is simply superior. But, contrary to U.S. popular belief, Europeans can make things that are worth buying, and they can sometimes make things which Americans cannot. The vertical takeoff aircraft is a case in point—yet it was with great reluctance, and only after many failures of its own aircraft, that the United States finally agreed to buy this equipment from Britain. Apart from psychological factors, there are also institutional obstacles, starting with the Buy American Act (there are no *Acheter France* or *Deutschland Kaufen* laws) and continuing with the manner in which defense contracts are awarded. Obstacles like these have to be overcome if the alliance is to move toward a different defense posture, and if its European members are to play their full part in doing so. The strains are familiar, but they are getting worse and stretching the fabric of the alliance tighter and thinner.

In all, the strategic guarantee is probably not endangered just because the U.S. commitment to Europe is now interdependent with the European commitment to the United States. The terms on which the guarantee could become endangered are those of the conflicting political, economic, and military interests of Europe and the United States. Can they be reconciled in the changing strategic and political context of Europe and of superpower relations?

That very question, however, raises a fundamental problem: the credibility of the U.S. strategic guarantee. Nobody knows, should hostilities break out, whether the president of the United States would actually be prepared to risk national suicide. In normal circumstances, that is enough to ensure security; precisely because nobody knows, the uncertainty presents a potential aggressor with dangers too great to calculate. But that very uncertainty is now being eroded. A former secretary of state, Henry Kissinger, said in a widely reported speech at the Palais d'Egmont that nuclear war was not possible. A former secretary of defense, Robert McNamara, wrote an article for *Foreign Affairs* in which he said that during his time in office he advised two successive presidents that in no conceivable circumstances should they ever resort to the use of nuclear weapons (McNamara added that he had every reason to believe that they both accepted his advice). When two such prominent Americans make declarations of that nature, the long-term credibility of the U.S. strategic guarantee must, to put it mildly, be increasingly open to question.

The problems indicated above are all of immediate import for the future of the alliance. NATO, if it is to survive, will need to move away from reliance upon the U.S. strategic guarantee and toward an understanding that the survival of the guarantee and the survival of the alliance are not the same. The survival of the alliance, the prime purpose of which is no longer to act as some kind of surrogate international order, remains essential to ensuring the defense of Western Europe. In other words, it is becoming a military alliance in a fairly narrow and classical sense—but in order to achieve that end, it is important that the member states reach agreement on burden sharing, economic matters, out-of-area questions, and the reorganization of relations with the Soviet Union at both the European and the superpower levels. That would make the alliance more effective and might even make the Europeans more self-reliant.

There are certainly ambitions in that direction. Early in 1987, the president of the European Commission, Jacques Delors, proposed a summit meeting on defense to be attended by the heads of government of the twelve community countries—this despite the fact that defense matters are *ultra vires* as far as the European Economic Community is concerned. Similarly, in early December 1987, the ministerial green light was given at NATO headquarters in Brussels for a related program: a NATO armaments planning system. The system was proposed in order to overcome the problems of the current process, in which national governments generally act independently until they run into trouble and need outside support. The proponents of the new plan hope to initiate NATO arms procurement projects and, eventually, establish a European procurement authority—an outgrowth, perhaps, of a body that already exists, the Independent European Programme. That body is, at present, only consultative, but it could become the basis for an authority with executive powers. Yet the obstacles are formidable.

At the moment, defense costs in Western Europe are increasing at a rate of 7 percent per year, well above the rate of inflation in most countries. And when one reflects that, even if costs rose only 2.5 percent per year, they would still double every quarter-century, one can see that it is simply not going to be possible to maintain procurement at existing levels. The incorporation of wildly expensive new technology accounts in large measure for the decline in procurement. To give one example, in the mid-1950s the U.S. aircraft industry was producing 3,000 combat aircraft per year. In 1987, it produced 159. But changes in the defense environment also increased costs. The INF treaty makes this very clear. The withdrawal of intermediate range nuclear weapons should logically imply a greater reliance on conventional defenses in Europe. But one point about nuclear weapons which has rarely been clearly enunciated is that they are dirt cheap, and thus have helped to keep defense costs relatively low throughout the post-war period. That is, in part, why NATO has been tempted to rely upon them. Consider a second example: It costs roughly the same either to build a nuclear weapon and keep it in an air-conditioned silo for one year or to maintain one tank with its crew of six and backup personnel for the same period of time. If conventional defense is to be substituted for the nuclear threat, one is driven to this irresistible conclusion: Either it is essential to engage in negotiations with the Soviet Union to achieve a more stable conventional balance in Europe, or else no member of NATO will be able to afford the kind of spending that would be needed to match Warsaw Pact forces. There is, of course, some comfort to be drawn from the fact that there is no need actually to match those forces tank for tank and gun for gun. The inherent advantages of conventional or nuclear defense are beginning to reassert themselves in conjunction with the great technological advances of recent years. But the fact remains that, without enormously increased NATO cooperation, minimal defense requirements will not be met.

But there is still a further obstacle to overcome in terms of increased cooperation. Mention has been made before of the two-way street and of U.S. disregard of the questions involved. But it is also true to say that the technology gap between Western Europe, on the one hand, and the United States and Japan, on the other, is steadily growing. One can see this quite clearly in the crucial sector of information technology. In 1960, Western Europe built 25 percent of all information technology equipment in the world. By 1983, that figure had diminished to 19 percent. It is down to 17 percent today, and by 1997, if present trends continue, Europe will contribute only 8 percent of the world's output in information technology. The gap in European technology trade is also mirrored in monetary terms. In 1987 that trade amounted to $15 billion, by 1992 projections indicate that it will be $30 billion, and, to extrapolate again, it will, by the turn of the century, be $45 billion by current standards. But the fact of the matter is that much of the focus for the development of information technology lies in military research, and it is in that area that the United States practices a form of blatant protectionism which should be the envy and admiration of the Japanese. The history of the Strategic Defense Initiative (SDI) contracts is a case in point. The memorandum of understanding exchanged between the United States and its European partners indicated that the research and development would be a joint transatlantic venture. But thus far, $5 billion have been spent in the United States on SDI research, out of which European companies have received only $50 million. The signs are that, out of the projected $26 billion research expenditure, the maximum that will come to European companies is $300 million. Congress likes it that way. The Glenn Amendment limits European access to SDI contracts if an American company is even remotely interested. The Traficanti Amendment actually seeks to impose an import surcharge when other countries sell defense equipment to America.

In short, the entire relationship needs restructuring. European defense cooperation is making some encouraging progress; but what is needed is a wider transatlantic relationship in which the United States comes to regard itself as a member of the alliance instead of continuing querulously to ask whether the Europeans are pulling their weight. Being a member of the alliance involves obligations as to sharing research and markets so as to make it economically feasible for Europeans to do more.

One need not despair here. The proportion of contribution on the two-way street added up to a 12 to 1 imbalance in favor of the United States at the beginning of this decade. By the mid-1980s it was down to 7 to 1; by 1987 it was only 2 to 1. But to retain or further reduce that 1987 level will probably require concerted policies, not only in terms of arms procurements but also in terms of the overall direction of research. A small beginning has been made with the earmarking of U.S. funds for investment in European defense cooperation, but a much bigger step could be taken if European companies received more than the 2 percent they currently enjoy of the annual U.S. defense equipment budget of about $100 billion.

The argument, therefore, is that while the obstacles are formidable, they can be overcome if the allies on both sides of the Atlantic are willing jointly to restructure their approach to common problems of defense. Otherwise there are two alternatives. One is continuing reliance on the U.S. strategic guarantee—and it has been here suggested that the credibility of the guarantee is in rapid decline and that, indeed, the survival of the alliance might depend upon its replacement. The second alternative is a new and excessive reliance on battlefield nuclear weapons stationed on West German soil. Nothing could be more calculated to ensure the rapid erosion of the alliance itself. It would maximize the problems outlined above and minimize the credibility of the readiness of the West to defend itself. If NATO has at last become a military alliance instead of a surrogate international order, then it is time that it should think and behave like one.

11

The Contribution of the Marshall Plan to Western Economic Development

HAROLD VAN B. CLEVELAND

When one speaks of the Marshall Plan, particularly if one was close to it and saw its results in its early years, hyperbole is natural. One need only consider the extraordinary speed of the European recovery and the subsequent growth of Western Europe, indeed of the whole West—not to mention the favorable evolution of the international economic order. On both of these levels, European recovery and the growth of the international order, it is difficult not to be impressed by the contributions of the Marshall Plan. Indeed, the enthusiasm and confidence aroused by the plan's success themselves explain, in part, that very success. But objectivity rather than enthusiasm is in order in this discussion.

An analytical examination of the recovery of Western Europe shows that Europe prior to the Marshall Plan was ripe for a powerful recovery. The supply of labor was large and elastic; unemployment and underemployment were high. In the Netherlands, where emigration to the colonies had been cut off, there was a large surplus of labor, as there was also in the French and Italian agricultural sectors. Even in Britain, where unemployment was statistically low, there was a great deal of underemployment due to controls and the rigidities of the British economy. The supply of labor in Europe was thus large relative to the existing stock of capital and of technology available from the United States.

These abnormal "factor proportions" set the stage for low labor costs, high profits, and high returns on investment. But an adequate current supply of investment resources was also needed to achieve high rates of European investment; this was provided by a high rate of personal savings and by foreign aid. Personal savings in Europe were high because households were rebuilding their wealth that had been depleted during the war. Business savings were high due to large profits. Interest rates were therefore low relative to investment returns, so that a high rate of investment and growth was possible. In short, the potential for high real growth was present; the problem was how to make this potential actual. That is where the Marshall Plan made a significant contribution.

The great economic problem for Western Europe after the war was the inability to cover the cost of imports. These countries had immediately after the war embarked on ambitious reconstruction programs. The question may be asked as to why the European governments thought that they would have enough resources to carry them out. It appears that, even before the Marshall Plan was proposed, there was an unspoken assumption that the United States would eventually make a great deal of aid available. The massive Western European balance of payments gap that emerged both in 1946 and in 1947 was primarily the result of the high level of domestic spending for reconstruction and new investment. The payments deficits were not due primarily to the bad harvest of 1947, though that was a contributing factor. The four-year Marshall Plan came forward at a critical time, assuring that additional resources would be available to sustain the momentum of the recovery that had already developed by 1948.

The rise of industrial production in 1948 for the participating Marshall Plan countries was an impressive 20 percent. This figure shows how rapidly both domestic demand and supply were expanding and, most particularly, how rapidly investment was expanding. Because the West European economies got enough foreign aid to cover the resulting balance of payments gap, they were lifted onto the high-growth path that they maintained through the 1950s and 1960s.

Was there an alternative to Marshall Plan aid? There is some truth to the revisionist argument that, through domestic stabilization efforts, some of the countries could have done without aid on the scale of the Marshall Plan. The argument may not fit the French case, but it clearly does fit the British case. But a great strain would have been put on all the countries had they been compelled to go through a drastic stabilization with monetary policy tightened, budget deficits slashed, and the recovery of production dependent mainly on exports.

Europe could have done it, but at high domestic cost. Investment and production would have recovered more slowly. The political cost in France or Italy might also have been high, with dangerous consequences. A major contribution of the Marshall Plan was the avoidance of so abrupt, so painful, and so potentially dangerous an adjustment.

Another important contribution of the Marshall Plan was the atmosphere of confidence it generated in Europe. This atmosphere of confidence was achieved by offering Europeans the opportunity to take advantage of the favorable underlying factor-cost relationship in order to achieve high investment and rapid productivity growth; as indicated, this growth continued throughout the next two decades. The promise of economic integration which the plan contained, the elimination of bilateral trading owing to regional payment arrangements, and the liberalization of trade within Europe combined to increase both investment efficiency and productivity, thereby opening up the vista of rapid economic growth which had begun to characterize Europe by the mid-1950s.

A factor in Europe's strong postwar recovery, for which the Marshall Plan should receive no credit, was the performance of the U.S. economy at that time. By the end of the 1950s, the United States had restored domestic price stability for the first time since before the war. The U.S. economy was growing vigorously, with only relatively brief pauses or recessions. U.S. price stability was "exported" to Europe as Europe's imports from the dollar area came to be freed from restrictions and European exchange rates came to be devalued and linked to the dollar.

Despite all this, pessimism lingered and many refused to see how well Europe was getting along. An example is the views about the "dollar gap." In the early 1950s, some people believed that Europe's shortage of dollars would be everlasting. They assumed that the problem could not be overcome by altering exchange rates, since European currencies had already been devalued against the dollar in 1949. In 1952, two years after the British balance of payments deficit had recovered so much that Britain had opted out of Marshall aid, the British treasury department was still arguing that in order to make sterling convertible, a structural dollar gap of some $5 billion per year had first to be closed by the United States through aid, by tariff cutting, and by pumping up domestic demand in the United States.

A second example of unwillingness to acknowledge success was the official response in Europe to the outbreak of the Korean War in June 1950. The initial economic impact of the war was a sharp, speculative rise in international raw materials prices. For a few months, the European balance of payments, particularly the dollar balance, fell back into a large deficit as import prices shot up. The dollar gap had gone down to about $1 billion in 1950, but it increased again in 1951 as an immediate result of the Korean War. The interpretation by the Organization for European Economic Cooperation (OEEC) of these events was that the severe 1951 deficit was the norm, demonstrating the existence of a large structural dollar gap, while the good 1950 figures were an aberration due to fact that the European countries had not been expanding their domestic demand rapidly enough. But by the middle of 1952, the dollar gap had almost disappeared again.

What about the plan's contribution to the postwar international

economic order? In 1946 and 1947, some State Department officers working on the Marshall Plan were convinced that its most
important contribution would be the economic integration of
Western Europe. They also saw this integration as the key to the
development of the larger international system projected at Bret-
ton Woods (the International Monetary Fund and the World
Bank), in the General Agreement on Tariffs and Trade (GATT),
and in the draft charter of the International Trade Organization.
In retrospect, I believe that, in the absence of economic integration in Europe—by which I mean the elimination of intra-
European trade quotas and the creation of a customs union—the
U.S. postwar vision of an open international trading system
would have been stillborn. It would have contributed nothing
but two institutional fossils: the International Monetary Fund and
the General Agreement on Tariffs and Trade.

Political scientists and economists have sometimes tried to
explain the emergence of the postwar international system as an
inevitable consequence of the increase of economic interdependence, which is, in turn, a function of economic growth in a capitalist or market system. This view is nationalistic, if not to say
essentially naive. The closer countries are to each other, the more
their affairs are entangled. This proximity creates an objective
common interest in maintaining openness and cooperation, but
it may also lead to conflict. The 1930s provide ample examples of
such ambiguities and tensions. Either order or disorder may result
from interdependence; which eventually emerges depends, above
all, on the quality of the values and the spirit that move the
national actors.

In other words, the objective common interests that economic
interdependence creates must be defined and made operational
by a certain farsightedness, a good deal of patience, some
accepted leadership, and a minimum of trust in the final intentions of the other actors. If these are lacking, common interest
will remain theoretical. None of these prerequisites for a successful international economic order is natural or inevitable. They
are all generally in short supply. We must regard their existence
in the postwar world as a remarkable political and moral achievement.

What did the Marshall Plan contribute to this achievement? On the institutional level, the plan created the practice of continuing multilateral dialogue—if you will excuse this contradictory expression—among the European governments and between them and the United States. Perhaps more importantly, on the level of values and ideology, it helped the European countries to develop economic policies conducive to, or at least consistent with, international integration. That outcome was by no means preordained. Ideologies of the left were dominant to one degree or another in Britain, France, and Italy at the end of the war. These ideologies projected economic regimes that would have made a highly integrated international system problematic, if not impossible. For the order that emerged to come to life, socialism in Western Europe had to be basically modified. It had to lose its excessively distributionist, interventionist, and protectionist aspects or simply be swept aside. Making that transition possible—making it ideologically respectable to the European consciousness—was an important contribution of the Marshall Plan.

The Marshall Plan was probably necessary and certainly beneficial. Economic recovery could probably have occurred with less aid. Orthodox economic stabilization programs could have been a partial substitute. But without the Marshall Plan, the economic recovery of Western Europe would have been severely impeded. The working international economic order that has done so much for prosperity and peace might never have come to be.

12

Germany and
the Marshall Plan

HERMAN ABS

After the German surrender in May 1945, I was asked by the British military government to advise on certain monetary and central banking problems facing Germany, much to the dislike of the Americans who did not, unlike the British, wish to reconstitute something of the past. The Americans had different ideas about the future of Germany, and some of these were still very close to the ideas of Henry Morgenthau, Jr.

I happened to own a book of Henry Morgenthau, Jr., which he dedicated to General Eisenhower on 2 October 1945; it was a reduced Morgenthau Plan for Germany to assist the president if, after the defeat of Germany, he might be in charge of her political future. This book was used as a guide by the United States in the war against Hitler and Nazi Germany, but it was never fully accepted, especially by Roosevelt. Nonetheless, the book became the standard work on how to deal with Germany after the unconditional surrender. It remained so until Joint Chiefs of Staff Directive 1067 poured what Henry A. Wallace once called ''a

considerable amount of water into the original Morgenthau acid.''
The Morgenthau ideas were finally disposed of by the famous
speech of Secretary of State James F. Byrnes in Stuttgart on 6
September 1946. The speech was considered by the U.S. press
and public to constitute a significant change in the attitude toward
Germany. This change occurred within sixteen months of the
German surrender.

Until the end of the war, I was a member of the board of general
managers of Deutsche Bank, a commercial bank that was often
considered the central bank in Germany. It is only by virtue of
having held this position that I am asked to speak in international
conferences. I was appointed to the board in September 1937.
Prior to that time, I was a private banker, a partner in an old
Berlin banking firm established in 1712.

The situation in May 1945 was a catastrophe. Germany was
grappling with physical devastation and political turmoil. Only a
few cities had escaped complete destruction. One of these was
Heidelberg, which had probably been selected by the U.S. forces
before the end of the war as an ideal place for the high command
of the victorious U.S. Army in Germany; the British were not as
precise in planning where they would set up shop after the defeat.
We were in total distress in Germany. This was particularly so
since the eastern part of Germany was occupied by Soviet forces
and already partially annexed by the Soviet Union (these annexed
areas included the eastern part of East Prussia or other lands
handed over, after the war, to Poland as compensation for territory the Poles had lost in the east to the Soviet Union as a result
of the prewar agreement between Stalin and Hitler). People were
fleeing this eastern part of Germany, including the part now call-
ing itself the German Democratic Republic. By 1951, almost ten
million refugees had come from the east to what has become the
Federal Republic of Germany.

The West German cities were nearly devastated. Cologne's
population alone had been reduced from 800,000 to 40,000 during
the war. As for the degree of destruction, there was a certain
amount of wagering going on over whether one's own or one's
neighboring city had been more devastated. This was a somewhat
cynical, but understandable, preoccupation of that period. Now,

if you consider the implications of ten million displaced people, you can easily imagine the postwar malaise in Germany.

Immediately after the occupation, the U.S. and British forces began to feed people. The total spending of the United States for food under the appropriation acts for Government and Relief in Occupied Areas (GARIOA) reached the equivalent of $1.6 billion. And the British, despite their wartime shortages and great manpower losses, added more than £250 million (then about $700 million) to feed and shelter displaced persons coming from the east.

At that time, German currency had no purchasing power. The unit of exchange you paid for labor was a U.S. cigarette; the going rate was about two cigarettes per hour. The purchasing power of the existing currency at that period was so close to zero that it was not acceptable to any labor forces. The monetary reform of 1948, a major accomplishment, was handled smoothly and successfully by the United States; it was so slick that no German assistant had any influence on the decision. It was the brainchild of the Americans, especially Tenenbaum and a few others who were later important consultants to the Central Bank of the Federal Republic of Germany.

It was in this atmosphere that the first announcement of a program intended to revitalize the economies of Western Europe was made. According to General George Marshall's own view, the plan originated in April 1947 during the Moscow Council of Foreign Ministers. The State Department's policy planning staff supported the idea; George Kennan, a great American and a great civil servant, contributed to the famous speech delivered by Marshall at the Harvard commencement in June 1947. The Marshall Plan was obviously designed to meet political objectives, despite its economic overtones.

The European Recovery Program included Allied countries such as the United Kingdom and France, as well as countries that were on the Allied side and had been occupied by Germany (the Netherlands, Belgium, Luxembourg). It also included the defeated nations—Germany, Austria, and Italy. (Italy had breached its alliance with Hitler in order to assist the U.S. forces landing in Italy.) The Marshall Plan was even designed to help rebuild the Soviet Union and its satellites. Stalin refused any assistance from the United

States under the Marshall Plan, because he believed he would ultimately be pressured by the West to make concessions to a future European settlement that would be unacceptable to him.

The Marshall Plan took effect quickly. At the same time, President Harry Truman, one of the great presidents, succeeded in two ways: he found a solution for the Far East by placing General Douglas MacArthur in Japan and he restored our confidence in the prospects for the democratic reconstruction of Europe. He sent a personal assistant, Richard Whitehead, perhaps a name unknown to you, to Frankfurt to see the U.S. military government representative and to find out more about Germany. Whitehead, an industrialist, wanted to know more about the actual situation in September 1947, especially in the economic sector. The U.S. military government officials told him that there were only a few people who could give him an answer: I was one of them. I don't know why I had this reputation. I must have been an innocent.

He stayed at my farm on the Rhine for two days in September. We discussed Marshall's proposal to include Germany in the assistance program. I told him that the plan was of great importance. A reconstruction program based solely on GARIOA supplies would not have been possible. All the goods being shipped from the United States to Germany were paid for by German importers. The problem was what to do with the equivalent of the imported goods. The cash dollar element in Marshall Plan aid was limited, while the Germans needed a great deal of assistance, especially with so many displaced persons coming into the country.

I proposed an institute that was established even before we had a federal government and a federal republic (those only came into being in 1949)—a Reconstruction Loan Corporation. The German translation is "Kreditanstalt für Wiederaufbau." In 1948, I was asked to organize this institution. We received the counterpart funds of Marshall Plan aid and certain remaining balances of GARIOA to be used as a revolving fund for the reconstruction of German industrial life. For this purpose, it was important to use the counterpart funds in the most effective way, and it was the task of Kreditanstalt to take care of this.

At that time, we had a bizonal administration near Frankfurt run by the U.S. military administration. Involved in the bizonal administration was a person of great importance for the postwar period: Ludwig Erhard. He believed in freedom and especially in a free market economy. One day, shortly after the monetary reform, when he was still a member of the bizonal administration for economics and finance, he was summoned by the military governor General Lucius Clay to answer one charge: "Erhard, you have done something you are not allowed to do: you changed military government law." Erhard replied, "I did not change anything." "But," the general countered, "you have to admit that you have lifted physical controls on production; you have lifted price controls on a number of articles in the German economy; you have opened the way to free action for industry and for hardworking business people. You cannot deny that you have changed military government law." So Erhard, in his innocence, said, "General, I didn't change anything, I only lifted the corresponding articles of military law." Clay, who became a very close friend of mine until the end of his life, told me that among his two most important achievements were the Berlin airlift and letting Erhard get away with having violated a number of military laws concerning price controls over the economy.

But there was one difficulty. Certain economic sectors still remained under controls: These sectors included coal, energy, water, agriculture, housing, and rents to be paid by people living in badly damaged houses. The cement factories built up new capacities, but they were not able to make use of them because there was no coal to make cement. This dilemma was recognized by the U.S. administration, and so they decided to make loans to those industries that produced basic goods such as coal.

The costs of producing coal were, at that time, DM 78 per ton, but pursuant to the military government controls the coal had to be sold to Switzerland for DM 16 per ton. The permanent loss of the coal mines had to be financed by credits, which is, in a free economy, the royal road to bankruptcy; but in a controlled economy, though you may allow for extended losses, you cannot permit bankruptcy. That was a situation well understood by both the Americans and the British. It was my idea to force those who had the privilege of freedom of action to loan DM 1.2 billion to basic industries that could not make investments in excess of the price they charged the consumer.

By 1953, we established an equilibrium between the development of the various industrial sectors and an unemployment rate that was, in spite of the great number of employed people coming from the east, less than one million and only about one-third of what it is today. That illustrates the tremendous influence of the U.S. administration, which often differed from that of the British. But British efforts have to be acknowledged, as do those of the French, in order to understand how we achieved reconstruction and rehabilitation. I believe that it was because of the magnanimous attitude of Marshall, backed by Truman and many people in the United States, that the future of Europe was changed.

There are some politicians and historians in my country who downplay the importance of Marshall Plan aid for what was later called the German "economic miracle." At that time, Germany had poor capital possibilities. I will give you an example. Clay, the military governor, said, "Abs, you must do something to find money in the capital market." So Kreditanstalt made an issue of a special loan paying 3.5 percent interest, free of income tax, free of property tax, free of inheritance tax, free of all taxes. You can imagine how many millions we sold.

There were some people in the board of Kreditanstalt who said: "But Abs, you are crazy. Kreditanstalt has no power to place any bond at issue in the capital market, at least in such a poor market as we have today." That was in 1949, still before we had a federal government, before there was the Federal Republic of Germany. And I replied, "Naturally we have no power to issue bonds. We are much too young as an institution. But you cannot call a man impotent because he has no children."

The total amount of this privileged loan was DM 8 million; it was a public issue, but in spite of its tax-exempt status, no buyers were found. We had a taxed, bonded issue especially for apartment-building construction which was issued at the same time, and the total amount placed was DM 35 million. Numerous banks helped to sell those bonds. That shows how poor the situation was immediately after monetary reform in Germany, and how important Marshall aid and the counterpart funds were for the rehabilitation and reconstruction of Germany. Under the German federal government, the distribution of Marshall Plan aid was taken over by Kreditanstalt. Up to the end of 1953, it distributed more than DM 6 million (90 percent of which were counterpart funds). All inflowing amounts were constantly reused on a revolving basis; this gave the institution the financial legitimation to carry out future tasks.

The use of counterpart funds differed in the various recipient countries. In Britain, these funds totaled about $8 billion, but they were not used for investment credits. Credit board government bonds were cancelled in order to counteract the inflationary effect of imports for which no payments were made. This was a traditional way to approach a different problem: Norway did the same thing, while France and Belgium also used counterpart funds, albeit with a certain hesitancy. The most classic form was established in West Germany. The level of counterpart funds used in France, for example, was about 20 percent larger than that of self-financed investments. Compared with this, the level of counterpart funds used in the same period in West Germany for the financing of industrial investments came to about 40 percent of the level of self-financed investments. This comparison not only shows the importance of the counterpart funds for France's industrial recovery, particularly in its steel industry, but also the importance of self-financing in Germany. By 1953, the various countries no longer needed Marshall Plan aid.

There is another important point: Without Marshall Plan aid, the European Economic Community, the European Coal and Steel Community, and, ultimately, the London Debt Agreement would not have been possible. Marshall Plan aid made it economically feasible for West Germany to negotiate its debts, including both the prewar debts of the German empire and the postwar debts of West Germany. These negotiations commenced in September 1950; the agreement was signed on 27 February 1953 and was ratified in September 1953. The regulation of external debts and the agreement of achievable repayment amounts ultimately reestablished German credit and led to the convertibility of the deutsche mark. That the annual sum of DM 567 million—later DM 765 million—agreed to by the creditor countries could be comfortably repaid out of export surpluses was due not least to Marshall Plan aid.

The London Debt Agreement settled the German indebtedness deriving from U.S. postwar economic assistance for a total of $1 billion. We had until 1987, but we repaid that sum in advance. The last repayment installment was made in 1967 out of our current account, thanks to the ability of the West German government to come up with the amount for payment. It was a great achievement of our minister of finance Fritz Schaffer, a Bavarian, who had the wonderful capacity, masterfully developed by Margaret Thatcher, to say "no." Credit must be given to him and to the federal government for repaying the Marshall Plan aid amounts from tax revenues and not from returning counterpart funds. These latter funds are used even today as a revolving fund for credit, especially for programs of development assistance for those Third World countries that need capital support.

I believe that I have explained what Marshall Plan aid meant to Germany. Would a Marshall Plan work for the developing world? I'm doubtful, because some of those developing countries must learn how to help themselves. They need a lot of physical assistance to boost production in agriculture and industry. The essential precondition for recovery, which we possessed in West Germany, was an industrious people skilled in industry and agriculture. We had about 4.3 million employable people, more than 2 million coming from the east. The only thing they needed was a chance to produce: a typical case of lack of capital. Under these circumstances, Marshall Plan aid could be a complete success. I believe nobody in my country who recognized the importance of Marshall Plan aid to Germany will ever forget its beneficial effect. Nor will they forget the attitude of the United States, Britain, and all those who fought the war against Germany to the bitter end, yet still displayed magnanimity to a defeated enemy, an unprecedented action so as to win Germany to the Atlantic Alliance.

We should never forget what Germans in this century have done in the name of Germany. We have no right to expect the world to forget. Above all, Germans have a duty never to forget.

13

The Changing Nature of the Soviet Threat

GEORGE H. QUESTER

Two questions are constantly before us: What has been the nature of the Soviet military threat to Western Europe since the end of World War II? And how has posing this threat served Soviet national interests?

In answering these questions, we will be trying to put ourselves into the shoes of Stalin and his successors, even as we actually remain in our own shoes as citizens of the NATO countries, concerned about the military and geopolitical vulnerability of Western Europe.

Related to such questions about Soviet capabilities and motivations is a parallel set of questions about U.S. capabilities and motivations. What kinds of threats have Truman and his successors been posing to the Soviet Union, deliberately or merely inevitably as a result of the emergence of U.S. military capabilities? These considerations close a circle. As in many international conflicts, each side's capabilities generate fears about the capabilities of the other.

We will continually ask ourselves a double-edged question on the Soviet threats to Luxembourg and the other democratically governed states of Western Europe. What might the Soviets actually want to do to this region? And what have they merely wanted *to be able to do* for purposes of deterrence?

The starting point for our concerns has been noted many times before: the outcome of World War II, which saw Soviet forces deployed throughout Eastern Europe and into the center of Germany. At least in terms of capability, this deployment seemed to confirm the worst geopolitical fears of Halford Mackinder.[1] The power that dominated the center of Eurasia was now posed to threaten military movement into the peninsulas sticking out as promontories from this center. If nothing else, this situation might be viewed as a replay of the nineteenth century "great game," when the British had to worry about the imperialist ambitions of czarist Russia. Would the Russians move against India, Scandinavia, China, or Turkey, or through the center of Europe? From the central position held by the czar's Russian empire, a position that Stalin had considerably enhanced by 1945, all such advances were possible. Soviet forces moving across the land would have a major logistical advantage over any opposing forces that had to be transported by sea or air.

With the stage thus set by capability, what could we sketch out as plausible Soviet motives? We begin with Eastern Europe.

Was Stalin's insistence on imposing pro-Moscow Communist regimes in Eastern Europe merely a nostalgic restoration of empire? Lithuania, Latvia, and Estonia were simply absorbed, along with Bessarabia, while Poland was subjected to a nominally independent Communist party regime that actually took orders from Moscow.[2]

Perhaps the Communist party regimes were imposed on Eastern Europe because of the dictates of ideology. Perhaps Stalin and his comrades sincerely wished well for the Poles, the Ruma-

---

[1]Halford J. Mackinder, *Democratic Ideals and Reality* (New York: W. W. Norton, 1962).

[2]Soviet post-1945 motives in Eastern Europe are discussed in Zbigniew Brzezinski, *The Soviet Bloc* (Cambridge, Mass.: Harvard University Press, 1967).

nians, and the Bulgarians and regarded Marxist political and economic regimes as the best way to advance human happiness.

Or perhaps the primary motive was a natural defensive Soviet concern that most of the East European regimes, if left to their own devices, would pursue foreign and military policies hostile to the Soviet Union. Only Czechoslovakia and Bulgaria had been friendly to Moscow before and during World War II (the Bulgarians, as allies of the Germans, had refused to declare war on the Soviet Union). If the Poles, Hungarians, and Rumanians were so viscerally anti-Russian, always seeking to join with Moscow's enemies to further their own territorial irredentist ambitions, then it would hardly have been paranoid for Stalin and his associates to want to establish a buffer of protection against them.

How then does this list of candidate motives translate into our concerns about Soviet intentions toward Western Europe? If Moscow's primary motive was simply a continuation of Russian imperialist dreams, then it was noteworthy that these dreams had reached beyond Warsaw in the past, and could still do so in the late 1940s and 1950s. This would be a classic power-politics interpretation. Any imperial power seeks to exploit opportunities to expand its domain.

The aforementioned postulates of ideology are an alternative explanation, but they do not diminish the concerns about Soviet intentions toward Western Europe. If the Polish workers had been rescued from the exploitation of capitalism by the Red Army and the Soviet secret police, might not the same benefits be appropriate for the workers of France, Italy, Luxembourg, and Belgium?

Finally, in terms of Moscow's most plausible fears of threats from the outside, we must turn to the other most notable happening of 1945, aside from the Soviet army's advance to the Elbe River and Eisenach: the introduction of nuclear weapons in the U.S. bombings of Hiroshima and Nagasaki. It is possible that a most important explanation of Soviet attitudes and capabilities toward Western Europe after 1945 stems simply from Moscow's elementary concern about what the United States would do with such atomic weapons when no one else had them (whether, that is, other countries might be beaten into submission as Japan had been).[3]

We must now ask some important basic questions about U.S. intentions. Perhaps the Soviets, ever since 1945, have felt an urgent need to threaten something of value to the United States, simply for deterrence.

We must ask a prior question, which now too often gets skipped over whenever we discuss arms control, nuclear deterrence, and nuclear duopoly: Why did the United States not use nuclear weapons against the Soviets between 1945 and 1949, the years when only the United States had such weapons and had no more reason to fear retaliation by the Soviets than by the Japanese? Why did the United States not pursue the course outlined by Bertrand Russell,[4] analogous to our policy toward Japan, by which nuclear weapons would have been used to impose surrender and disarmament and democratization on what had been a threat to world peace? Why was the U.S. nuclear monopoly not used to perpetuate itself? Our policy with regard to Japan had been paradoxically straightforward: namely, that one Japanese city would be destroyed every three days, until Tokyo agreed to establish free popular elections in these cities, after which a very benign intrusion of American influence would soon enough be revealed.

All of this is not completely irrelevant to today's discussions of strategy, of course. Former president Reagan's Strategic Defense Initiative (SDI) proposal would, at least in Reagan's own original formulation, have returned the world to a situation like that of 1947, when U.S. cities were secure against Soviet nuclear attack.[5] Perhaps Soviet cities would quickly thereafter be offered the same protection, as the world returned to the situation of 1944. But, the Soviets can reasonably ask, what would keep Washington from using its monopoly of a nuclear threat against cities if it,

[3]On Soviet intentions toward Western Europe, see Herbert Feis, *From Trust To Terror* (New York: W. W. Norton, 1970).

[4]A detailed discussion of Bertrand Russell's advocacy of preventive war can be found in Ronald William Clark, *The Life of Bertrand Russell* (London: Jonathan Cape, Weidenfeld and Nicholson, 1975), chap. 19.

[5]For President Reagan's own version of the intended goals of the SDI, see the *New York Times*, 24 March 1983, p. 1.

through the SDI, attained such a monopoly? Americans might then point to the experience of 1945–49 as the vouchsafe of their good intentions.

When asked to account for this strange passing of a military monopoly, U.S. students often assume that this was due to a special U.S. political morality (the United States under President Truman would have been incapable of beginning a war).[6] It took the Japanese attack on Pearl Harbor, by this interpretation, to produce Hiroshima and Nagasaki. A combination of morality and naivete, uniquely American, allowed the nuclear monopoly to become the nuclear duopoly we tend to take so much for granted now in all of our discussions of mutual deterrence and the "balance of terror."

Yet such a picture of special naivete—by which the United States let a unique opportunity pass by—or of special morality— by which Americans are an unusually peace-loving people—is not unanimously accepted by analysts around the world today. Was it really impossible for a U.S. national leadership to see the opportunities and power possibilities here, and to be realistic and Machiavellian about exploiting them? The model of Roosevelt's handling of relations with Japan before Pearl Harbor might have suggested that Truman, given the many egregious Soviet violations of promises and the elementary dictates of political democracy in Poland and elsewhere in Eastern Europe in 1945, should provoke a major military confrontation with Stalin.

Other explanations, less critical of U.S. naivete or less flattering to U.S. morality, would turn to U.S. overconfidence in the duration of the nuclear monopoly (almost no one expected that Stalin would have atomic bombs of his own by 1949). A close look at the facts also shows that the United States produced very few atomic bombs in 1945–47, so that the U.S. "nuclear threat" to Moscow may have been largely a bluff.[7] Yet this begs the same questions that we have been raising here: Why did the United

[6]The argument that U.S. nonuse of nuclear weapons in these years is to be traced to American morality can be found already in Bernard Brodie, ed., *The Absolute Weapon* (New York: Harcourt Brace, 1946).

[7]On the size of the U.S. stockpile, see David Alan Rosenberg, "U.S. Nuclear Stockpile, 1945 to 1950," *Bulletin of the Atomic Scientists* 38 (May 1982): 25–30.

States not keep the requisite physicists and nuclear engineers in place to ensure that a sizable U.S. nuclear weapons stockpile would be at hand?

Some analysts might argue that it would have been impossible to force a democratization and demilitarization of the Soviet Union, citing the alleged lessons of Vietnam and of much of the past two decades of U.S. foreign policy. After all, there is very little that one can do to change the political and social and military inclinations of the outside world. Yet an equally ambitious task was undertaken by the United States in 1945 with regard to Japan and West Germany; despite all the later cliches to the effect that democracy and the U.S. style of political life can never be exported, these efforts seem to have succeeded. Perhaps the United States could have done a great deal of good for the world if it had followed Russell's advice in the early postwar years, making a nuclear war impossible (since no one else would have been allowed to develop such weapons), enriching the lives of Soviets and East Europeans, and making Western Europe secure against all the threats we are listing here.

But, to return to our main theme, the most cynical and power-oriented student of international relations will not accept any such theory of U.S. naivete and morality to explain why U.S. atomic bombs were not used against Stalin in 1946 or in 1948. The student would instead argue that the U.S. nuclear threat was countered effectively by the Soviet conventional military capability for advancing into Western Europe. If Truman had tried to apply the nuclear monopoly to perpetuate itself, or to force democracy on the Soviet Union, one Soviet city a week might have been destroyed by the U.S. Air Force (never Moscow, of course, since its ability to surrender might have been crucial, just as it would have been a disaster for the United States to have dropped its first atomic bomb on Tokyo, for this would—unlike the conventional bombings of that city—have killed the emperor), but Soviet ground forces would in the meantime have occupied Frankfurt, Copenhagen, Luxembourg, and Paris.[8]

[8]See Lawrence Freedman, *The Evolution of Nuclear Strategy* (New York: St. Martin's, 1981), p. 52.

Perhaps it was, as Winston Churchill argued in March 1949, only the threat of U.S. nuclear weapons which kept Soviet ground forces from advancing to the Bay of Biscay. Or only (at least as seen from Moscow) the threat of such an advance which kept U.S. nuclear weapons from being dropped on Soviet cities.

If a Soviet conventional grip on Western Europe confronted Washington with a potential retaliation that Americans would always have regarded as unacceptable, then that threat was replaced, after 1949, by the prospect of a Soviet *nuclear* grip on all of the same cities of Western Europe. At the same time that Stalin was pushing for the earliest possible production of atomic bombs for the Soviet Union, he had also produced carbon copies of the U.S. B-29. With some 700 such Soviet Tu-4 bombers being readied, Stalin was surely endangering Britain and the entire European continent, though these planes were probably incapable of carrying nuclear warheads as far as North America.[9]

While British analysts had not been particularly averse to various possible uses of U.S. nuclear weapons in response to Soviet threats prior to 1949, they had taken a drastically different tack by 1950, when Truman was led to speculate about a possible use of nuclear weapons in the Korean War. These speculations precipitated an immediate uproar in the British parliament. (Prime Minister Clement Atlee flew to Washington to obtain assurance from Truman that no such action was being contemplated.[10])

By the end of the 1950s, the attention of British and American analysts had shifted to the imminent development of ballistic missiles. They would supplement or replace manned-bomber aircraft as the way of delivering nuclear warheads to any target. For a time it was feared that the Soviets would acquire a unique capability in such intercontinental-range ballistic missiles (ICBMs), generating a "missile gap." Such missiles could threaten all of the U.S. bomber bases. This missile gap in favor of the Soviet Union did not materialize, for the Soviets were unable to fulfill

[9]On the Soviet development of nuclear weapons and delivery systems for such weapons, see David Holloway, *The Soviet Union and the Arms Race* (New Haven: Yale University Press, 1984).

[10]The Truman-Atlee meeting on the nuclear issue in Korea is discussed in Dean Acheson, *Present at the Creation* (New York: W. W. Norton, 1969), pp. 479–82.

Khrushchev's boast that ICBMs would be produced and deployed like "sausages." But it might be a mistake to regard this transition from the 1950s to the 1960s as a "missile gap in reverse."[11] The United States did suddenly find itself with an arsenal of ICBMs far outnumbering and outclassing those of the USSR, but the Soviets had managed to achieve quantity production of the SS-4 and SS-5 missiles, and intermediate-range vehicles again threatened the cities of Western Europe.[12]

In the next decade, Moscow's grip on Western Europe became redundant. The Soviets finally went past their difficulties with the quantity production of intercontinental-range missiles and submarine-based missiles (SLBMs) in the middle of the 1960s. These missiles now posed a threat to U.S. cities and not merely to U.S. interests in or near the continent of Europe. Since the 1960s, it has no longer been necessary for Americans to identify with remote West Europeans in order to understand why the United States is not free to use its nuclear weapons against the Soviet Union.

The SS-20 missile, configured as a replacement for the SS-4 and SS-5 missiles, would have to be seen as more redundant than these earlier missiles if the assigned task is that of deterring the United States. For the SS-20 can only destroy European cities that could be destroyed as well by Soviet ICBMs fired on a short trajectory; but, at the same time, those Soviet ICBMs can destroy the cities of the United States.

An important point needs to be made about what the Soviets must have assumed through all these decades as to the U.S. commitment to Western Europe. If Moscow felt that it needed to be able to occupy Western Europe with its tank forces, or to be able to destroy Western Europe with its medium-range rocket forces, as a way of deterring U.S. nuclear capabilities, then this already imputed (in Soviet calculations of U.S. motivations) the status of the "fifty-first state" to places like Luxembourg. Pierre

---

[11]On the "missile gap in reverse," see Desmond Ball, *Politics and Force Levels* (Berkeley: University of California Press, 1980).

[12]The quantity deployment of SS-4 and SS-5 missiles is discussed in Thomas W. Wolfe, *Soviet Power and Europe: 1945–1970* (Baltimore: Johns Hopkins University Press, 1970), pp. 183–84.

Gallois,[13] and many others since, have argued that the United States will not care enough about West Germany, France, and other NATO members to be willing to defend them or to escalate to nuclear warfare on their behalf, and that the Soviets will quickly see a yawning gap in the credibility of U.S. commitments here. Yet the relationships just noted suggest that the Soviets have for decades now been *counting upon* a close U.S. identification with Western Europe as their own reliable back-up for deterrence; one cannot so easily have his cake and eat it here (a fifty-first state for one purpose might easily be the same for another).

One can also ask what the impact would be of any real success for Reagan's version of the SDI. Rather than returning us to 1948, we might indeed be returned to 1951, with a *slight* chance that one U.S. city or another would be destroyed by way of a maximum Soviet effort to inflict some retaliation, and with a *great* chance that European cities would be destroyed. Here it would again make sense for Moscow to treat Western Europe as a hostage for U.S. good behavior, by posing the threats of either conventional occupation or nuclear destruction. Here the SS–20 would once more serve some real strategic purposes for the Soviets (rather than merely being a very redundant—and politically irritating—remnant of an ICBM for which the third stage did not pan out).

It must be stressed, however, that despite the shifts in Soviet nuclear capability, the conventional and geopolitical capabilities that Moscow can direct at Western Europe still remain in place. Ever since the end of World War II, the Soviets have maintained tank totals far larger than those they face west of the Elbe. Any such military vehicles with wheels and tracks compound the geopolitical dilemma posed by the interior position of the Soviet Union. So the Soviet ability to occupy Europe remains worrisome. This is so even if that capability no longer seems needed to counter U.S. nuclear capabilities, for the Soviet ability to destroy Western Europe by nuclear means remains in place as well.

[13]Pierre Gallois, *The Balance of Terror* (Boston: Houghton Mifflin, 1961).

The stage is now set for our analytical discussions. It is set with policies that the Soviets would never want to do for their own sake (such as a nuclear destruction of Western Europe), but might well have wanted to be *able* to do. It is also set with things that we cannot be so certain that the Soviets would never want to do (such as a conventional "liberation" of Western Europe).

The argument that says the Soviets have no reason to fire SS–20 missiles, or any other nuclear weapons, at Luxembourg or at Copenhagen is simple enough. The winds blow from west to east for most of the year, and the radioactive fallout would soon enough degrade life in the Soviet Union as well. And the Soviets surely do not look forward to conquering and bringing the "benefits" of communism to radioactive cities.

The argument that says the Soviets desire, or do not desire, conventional conquest of Copenhagen and Luxembourg and all of Western Europe is much more difficult to sort out; it has been difficult to do so since 1945. Some revisionist analysts can convince themselves that Stalin would never have let his Red Army occupy Paris, even if the United States had not possessed nuclear weapons, for fear of what would happen to such troops once they had seen the luxuries of the West.[14] Yet an easy counterargument would point to the charm and affluence of Budapest, and the fact that the Soviets have not (yet) been so perverted and subverted by this exposure to Western styles of civilization.

Where the Soviet ground-advance capabilities remain in place, even after they have become redundant with respect to any deterrent defensive purposes, one finds nourishment again for our concerns about possible Soviet offensive purposes. Do the Soviets not believe their own propaganda about the masses being so badly off in Western Europe and so much better off in Eastern Europe? If they do believe that, the stage is set for Western fears of a use of Soviet conventional (but not nuclear) capabilities.

By posing two hypothetical counterhistorical possibilities, one can rephrase our analytical exercise here once more.

---

[14]A more contemporary argument about why Moscow would never want to send its troops into Western Europe is outlined in Richard J. Barnet, "Why On Earth Would the Soviets Invade Europe?" *Washington Post*, 22 November 1981, pp. C1–2.

First, what would Stalin have done after 1945 if there had been *no* nuclear weapons in the world? This is the question that has been bedeviling Europe since the Marshall Plan.

Second, what would Stalin have done if *he* alone had possessed nuclear weapons after World War II? On this latter question, I am convinced that the Soviet nuclear monopoly would have been preserved, such that the world would today have no worries about thermonuclear war. I am also convinced that this chapter would be written in Russian on the topic of the advantages of socialism, and that it would be subject to an editorial stylebook forbidding the juxtaposition of "Soviet" and "threat." There would have been a Marshall Plan, but it would have taken a very different, more compulsory form, with much more U.S. wealth crossing the Atlantic, and most of it being channeled east of the Elbe.

When such thoughts and inclinations can be plausibly imputed to Stalin, they can be attributed to nearly the same degree to any statesman, so that a similar imputation about Truman certainly had to have had credibility with Stalin.

In light of all this background on Soviet capabilities and possible Soviet fears of American and European capabilities, what form of Soviet attack has been dreaded by the West from year to year and decade to decade?

Was there an immediate conventional military threat to Western Europe? In some ways, yes, and in others, no. The geopolitical advantages of the Soviet position achieved in 1945 have already been noted. The Soviets were also very plausibly seen as having an advantage both in the larger potential populations that could be mobilized for land combat (this sense of "Asian hordes" was augmented after 1949 by the Chinese Communists) and in the total societal and personal discipline that could be achieved in a police state.

Giving the West some respite, for an undetermined time, was the severe economic damage inflicted by the German attack on the Soviet Union and the obvious Soviet need for rebuilding and recovery. The Red Army was somewhat disarmed after the German and Japanese surrenders, but far less so than was the U.S. Army.

As noted, Churchill had opined in 1949 that the Soviet conventional military threat to Western Europe was being held in check only by the counterthreat of U.S. nuclear weaponry. When the Soviets had no such weapons of their own, Britishers from Churchill to Russell had fewer compunctions about seeing (at least the threat of) the U.S. nuclear monopoly applied (keeping the Red Army from the Bay of Biscay and the English Channel seemed to be a good thing).

By 1946–47, and especially by the beginning of 1948, the British fear had shifted more immediately to the dangers of an economic and social collapse of Western Europe.[15] The wartime destruction had taken some time to achieve its fullest impact. By 1947–48, there existed the possibility that this general human suffering could be exploited sufficiently to bring Communist parties to power in Italy, France, and West Germany through some combination of strikes, violence, sabotage, and genuine election victories. This was the time when Maurice Thorez, the leader of the French Communist party, declared to the National Assembly that the French workers would welcome the Red Army as liberators.[16] This was also the time when Czechoslovakia was taken over by the "workers' militias" of the Communist party without any participation by Soviet forces, which remained across the border in Hungary and Poland.

We often forget the latent appeal of Marxist ideology and Communist parties in much of Europe. These parties win substantial minority slices of the vote even today in Finland, Sweden, and Norway. Similarly, they did quite well in the genuinely democratic processes of Czechoslovakia prior to 1948. In 1948 Washington was concerned that the Communist parties of France or Italy might actually win power in a free election (after which the system would be made like that of Eastern Europe, so that the Communists would never have to win another such electoral contest).

[15]On the economic and social problems of 1947 and 1948, see Joseph Jones, *The Fifteen Weeks* (New York: Viking, 1955).
[16]The Thorez statement is recounted in the *New York Times*, 23 February 1949, p. 1.

This latent appeal of the Communist parties in Europe stems from genuine class issues, as well as from the real dissatisfactions of many industrial workers and other voters with their lot in life. But this appeal is in turn reduced by a common perception of how the Communist parties have behaved in the Soviet Union and in Eastern Europe. The arrogance of the governing Communists in demanding total power, where they have been entitled at best to only a majority role, or more probably to a hefty minority role, has thus reduced the minority vote that Communist parties win today in Belgium, Luxembourg, West Germany, or France. This perception of Communist party arrogance goes along with our awareness of the constant threat of a conventional forward move by Soviet military forces. After all, they brought the Communists to power in much of Eastern Europe in the first place, and they are the principal maintainers of such power today.

In effect, we thus may have a "Finlandisation in reverse" here. The normal concern about Finlandisation is that ordinary people and governments in Western Europe will be intimidated by the visibility of Soviet tank-force potential, and thus subtly brought around into doing things more in the way that Moscow desires. But perhaps the specter of Soviet military power has been working just the other way around in West European polling booths, reducing the Communist vote.

The Marshall Plan was, of course, a response to such fears that West European economic and social deterioration might bring Communist parties to power by basically nonmilitary means. (The plan was also a very generous decision by the United States to work for economic and social recovery in Europe simply for its own sake.) The Marshall Plan was a glowing success as the West German and West European "economic miracles" took off after 1948, ending any real fears that cold or hunger would thereafter produce a communization of Europe.[17]

Yet our memory of the irreducible appeal of Communist party electoral campaigning in the 1940s still nourishes some of the fears we still carry with us today. Because there were some French

[17]On the fuller ramifications of the Marshall Plan, see Charles P. Kindleberger, *Marshall Plan Days* (Boston: Allen and Unwin, 1987).

workers, and others throughout Western Europe, who would have welcomed the Soviet tank forces as liberators, it is easier for the Soviets to see themselves as liberators. Because Communist ideology is not totally out of touch with the realities of life west of the Elbe, it would be easier for someone in Moscow to take that ideology seriously enough to send tanks across the Elbe.

What we have most to fear, to repeat, may not be Soviet imperialism, or Soviet self-interest, but rather Soviet ideology and Soviet generosity. If any Soviet leader since World War II had sent his tank forces racing toward Brussels or Luxembourg, it is all too possible that he would have convinced himself that this move would improve the quality of life and the degree of happiness in such cities.

It is often observed that Soviet forces had not invaded a national boundary until the invasion of Afghanistan in 1980. Defenders of the Soviet system, trying to reassure West Europeans, stress that Afghanistan and Central Asia are very different from Western Europe. Yet the ideological counterpoint has to be made. If Moscow can see itself bringing its correct version of socialism to even as backward a place as Afghanistan, could it not (in light of the teachings of Marx and Engels and Lenin) feel itself much more justified in doing the same for Denmark or Austria?

Here we are definitely dealing with what the Soviets might want to do for its own sake, out of a sense of "international socialist duty" and a feeling that they were contributing to the welfare of others. This is to be distinguished from the nuclear threats posed by the TU-4 and the SS-4, SS-5, and SS-20 missiles, which represent what the Soviets may merely feel compelled to be able to do as a preparation for tit-for-tat deterrence.

If the Soviet Union were simply a state governed by narrow, selfish interests, and if the United States were also such a state, there might be far less conflict between the two superpowers. Under such circumstances, Moscow might not be nearly so concerned about imposing communism on Poland, Hungary, or Czechoslovakia against the preferences of the majority of the people who live there. Moscow has convinced itself, perhaps ever since 1917, that the majority in Eastern Europe, and probably in all of Europe, wants, or appropriately deserves, socialism. This is what breathes life, even today, into the "Soviet threat."

The Soviet threat again became militarily plausible after 1949, for the Soviets now had their own atomic bomb; and this, by a very straightforward analysis, might cancel out the deterring impact of U.S. atomic bombs, restoring relevance to the Soviet conventional-force advantages. Such an analysis was already outlined in NSC–68,[18] a U.S. National Security Council document commissioned by Truman in the immediate aftermath of the first detection of a Soviet nuclear weapons test. A seeming confirmation of Western fears then emerged in the 1950, when North Korean tanks produced in the Soviet Union rolled so quickly across the border to spread the benefits of communism to all of Korea.

The threat loomed larger now, not only because of the Soviet acquisition of nuclear warheads, but also because of the much more urgent Soviet economic recovery from World War II destruction that had presumably been completed. While much of the Red Army had been demobilized in 1945, its fighting capacities were again on the upgrade in 1949–50, and a substantial expansion had also been undertaken in the satellite armies of the Communist-governed countries of Eastern Europe.

These were still the years in which Moscow's strong suit seemed to be the possibilities of conventional warfare. Before Moscow had obtained its own nuclear arsenal, a great propaganda effort had been devoted to the so-called Stockholm Peace Petition,[19] which proposed the ultimate abolition of all nuclear weapons, while forbidding their use in the interim. In the mid-1950s, the Soviets allowed the foreign minister of Poland to put forward the Rapacki Plan. It called for a "nuclear-free zone" across the middle of Europe—including Poland, Czechoslovakia, and both East and West Germany—within which all powers would promise never to use such weapons. Then, as now, the Western critics of such proposals could counter that their impact was simply to "make Europe safe for conventional war" (by mak-

[18]The text of NSC-68 was published in *Naval War College Review* 27 (May–June 1975): 51–158.

[19]On the Stockholm Peace Petition, see the *New York Times*, 30 March 1950, p. 3.

ing it possible for Moscow to send its conventional forces forward in some sudden coup, or perhaps simply to intimidate anti-Communist political forces by the mere prospect of such an attack).

If moves like the Rapacki Plan, which tended to delegitimize the presence or the use of nuclear weapons, seem to make perfect sense in terms of Soviet interests, then there could be difficulty in explaining certain periods in which the Soviets have stressed, in the event of any war in Central Europe, the likelihood of an escalation to nuclear exchanges.

One partial explanation might have emerged at the end of the 1950s. Then the major focus of East-West confrontation was over a militarily anomalous situation, the enclave of West Berlin. Here the Soviets would not have had to be the first party to take the conventional military initiative, for they could have cut off West Berlin simply by disabling road and rail connections and by jamming navigational systems for air travel. Hence it would have been up to NATO to initiate conventional warfare by attempting to send a relief column down the autobahn.

The threat of nuclear escalation generally discourages any initiation of conventional military initiatives; this is the most basic fact of life we have to work with here. In this special case, it would have been the Soviets who would have benefited from the nuclear escalation possibility, and the West that would have suffered from it.

Yet one finds references in the literature to a quick Soviet escalation to nuclear warfare in Europe even on into the 1970s, long after the Berlin Wall had solved the East German problem of controlling its population (the East no longer needed to exert pressure for a surrender of the West Berlin enclave).[20] Here there is a greater puzzle: For what was being reported by the analysts of Soviet military journals and maneuvers—that Moscow planned to use its own nuclear weapons, including the new SS-20, from

[20]For interpretations stressing Soviet readiness to use nuclear weapons in tactical combat situations, see Joseph D. Douglass, Jr., and Amoretta Hoeber, *Conventional War and Escalation: The Soviet View* (New York: Crane Russak, 1981).

the start of any war in Europe—flies in the face of all we have presented here as a plausible rendition of Soviet interests.

At the beginning of the 1980s, one at last obtains some semblance of a solution to this puzzle. The latest scanning of Soviet military journals and maneuvers now suggests that the Soviets were indeed rehearsing for both contingencies—a war fought with nuclear weapons in Europe and a war fought without—but were contemplating the former only reluctantly. Their reason for contemplating the nuclear option was that they accepted the likelihood that NATO would go through with its own threats of an early nuclear escalation.[21]

Each such scanning of the evidence of Soviet military inclinations has been put forward with some alarm (many of the scanners seem to think they must always sound alarms). In the 1970s, the message was that the Soviets would do us ill by rapid recourse to nuclear weapons. In the 1980s, the message is that they will seek to do us ill by a rapid advance without the use of nuclear weapons, even using their own conventional forces to try to preempt Western nuclear weapons.

Consistent with our analysis here, the Soviet nonnuclear advance plan has always made more sense for almost any rendering of Moscow's interests than do any plans for a nuclear attack on Europe. The basic points here remain the same. Once the Soviets have the ability to retaliate with nuclear weapons against the continental United States itself, their ability to inflict nuclear damage on Western Europe becomes redundant. The Soviet desire to inflict nuclear damage on Western Europe for its own sake is nonexistent.

The Soviets have seemingly never regarded the peoples of West Germany or of Luxembourg in the way that Hitler and the Nazis seem to have felt toward the Russians and the Jews. Our most serious worry is still whether Moscow feels the same toward West Germany and Luxembourg as it feels toward East Germany and Bulgaria. If Moscow still feels that it has a duty to spread socialism to all of Europe, we still have a Soviet threat.

---

[21]An analysis outlining the Soviet reluctance to see nuclear weapons used in a conventional war in Europe is presented in Phillip A. Peterson and John G. Hines, "The Conventional Offensive in Soviet Theater Strategy," *Orbis* 27 (Fall 1983): 695–740.

Therefore, one must question the value of the agreements signed by Gorbachev and Reagan in December 1987. The agreements essentially traded away Soviet nuclear missiles, with ranges capable of reaching only Western Europe, for American nuclear weapons systems based in Western Europe capable of reaching targets in the Soviet Union and Eastern Europe.

Only the citizen who pays very little attention to the details of these issues would see this as a symmetrical tradeoff. The Pershing II and the U.S. ground-launched cruise missiles (GLCMs) were not really required to counter the Soviet SS-20 or any other Soviet nuclear weapons systems. As stressed throughout this account, they were in place to counter the conventional threat of Soviet tanks.

A functionally more useful trade would have swapped Western missile reductions for Soviet tank reductions rather than missiles for missiles. The political symbolism of the reductions negotiated in December 1987 cannot be denied. It has value in its own right. Like much political symbolism, however, it bears little relationship to the reality of the issues.[22]

The Soviets are giving up larger numbers of missiles in agreeing to the SS-20 elimination, and some spokesmen for the Reagan administration claimed that the swap was a very good deal for the West. Yet the SS-20 had become an embarrassment for the Soviet leaders, again largely because of a political symbolism with no basis in reality.

The SS-20 is basically two-thirds of what originally had been designed to be the SS-16 intercontinental-range missile. Because the SS-20 is thus limited in range, it arouses ire, or at least protestations of ire, whenever its deployment is shifted, for this then deletes or adds to the targets it can strike. When deployed west of the Urals, it gave European leaders occasion to complain, even though the Soviet Union could deliver nuclear weapons against all the European cities by many other means. When shifted east of the Urals, it became the turn of the Japanese and the Chinese diplomats to complain on the same symbolic and nonsubstantive

[22]For an argument questioning the Gorbachev-Reagan agreement on nuclear weapons in Europe, see Colin Gray, "In Pursuit of START, We're Commiting Familiar Sins," *Los Angeles Times*, 15 December 1987, p. IV6.

grounds (again, there are many ways for the Soviets to hit Japanese or Chinese or Alaskan cities with nuclear weapons aside from the SS-20). If the SS-20 had become the SS-16, thus making all of these locations targetable all the time, then none of these diplomats would have seized upon these occasions to lodge protests in Moscow. Under these circumstances, Gorbachev might well have resented his predecessors' decisions to try to salvage two out of the three rocket stages of the failed SS-16, and might further have welcomed an opportunity to get rid of the system.

No one is now safe against nuclear attack in Western Europe, or elsewhere, just because the SS-20 has been eliminated. The trickier question is whether the residents of the Soviet Union are now somewhat safer against Western nuclear escalation, and whether the cities of Western Europe are somewhat less safe against Soviet tank attack. Here is where the critics of the Reagan-Gorbachev "double-zero" agreement make their strongest arguments.

Those who view the 1987 accords favorably would have to stress the broader political process now under way. Gorbachev may be able to use this kind of accord to liberalize his own country, and, as a result, Soviet ideological self-confidence, arrogance, and military threat may be reduced.[23] In fairness, the Soviets have been, in two successive annual meetings of the Warsaw Pact, considerably more forthcoming about addressing our Western concerns over conventional warfare capabilities (the very foundation of all our "asymmetries" and "geopolitical and historical" worries) and have indicated that they are ready to reduce the enormous numerical advantage they have in tanks and other weapons of mobile conventional warfare. If such is the case, then some very serious relief for our problems may be in sight.[24]

If the core of the problem lies in the number of Soviet tanks, then why has Moscow invested so heavily in this kind of military

[23]An argument stressing the political advantages of the Reagan-Gorbachev summit agreement can be found in Gerard C. Smith, "The INF Treaty: A Reason for Hope," *Arms Control Today* 18 (January–February 1988): 3–5.

[24]Leon V. Segal, "Conventional Arms In Europe: Signs of a Soviet Shift," *Bulletin of the Atomic Scientists* 43 (December 1987): 16–20.

vehicle, which favors the advance force in the event of crises and wars and which might one day trigger "a war nobody wanted"?[25] There are several theories as to why the Soviets have purchased so many armored vehicles that so outnumber the totals for NATO.

U.S. military commanders are typically envious of the numbers of tanks and of armored vehicles assigned to each 10,000 Soviet soldiers. They use this as an argument for matching increases in such deployments for NATO. If pressed on whether they would like to have just as high a density of armored vehicles for each 10,000 U.S. or NATO soldiers, however, they typically suggest that the Soviets have become "tank happy" since World War II, overloading themselves with more armored equipment than makes sense.

A first explanation of this Soviet commitment, or overcommitment, to armored warfare would stem from the memories of World War II, when the final repulse of the German attack amounted to a rolling defense. That was because static defenses had failed, while the vast land area of the Soviet Union lent itself readily to tank maneuvers and counterattacks. Here we have a magnificent reinforcement of a maxim that many military officers employ somewhat mindlessly to brush off any and all distinctions between offensive and defensive weapons: "The best defense is a good offense." The Soviets produced perhaps the best tanks in the world in World War II, and the battle of Kursk probably remains the largest tank battle in history. It would be unreasonable to expect the Soviets to abandon their military traditions and their natural confidence in armored warfare as a means of protecting their motherland.

A second possible explanation for the huge Soviet armored forces is the one that has concerned us so much: The Soviet leadership looks forward to bringing the benefits of a more revolutionary socialism to places like Luxembourg. What better way to prepare to liberate Maurice Thorez and his followers than an army highly trained in mobile conventional war?

A third explanation would point at Eastern Europe and at Mos-

---

[25]On the possible explanations for the massive totals of Soviet tanks, see Wolfe, *Soviet Power*, chaps. 17 and 18.

cow's continuing concerns over unrest in all of its satellites. As demonstrated in Hungary in 1956, and in Czechoslovakia in 1968, the tank is a very tangible means of dampening the enthusiasms of those who seek to oust Communist regimes. We shall speculate later about the future of Eastern Europe, for this area of unrest more generally affects Soviet inclinations and potential threats.

A final explanation of Soviet tank production would focus far less on such rational arguments and instead note that production in the Soviet Union has generally not been well-geared to needs. In one year the consumer gets size-ten shoes; the next year he gets size-twelve shoes, depending entirely on which factories solve the problems of getting their assembly lines working. Perhaps the Soviets have simply mastered the production of tanks at some point, and the result is that Soviet forces are equipped with large numbers of them. (In fairness to the Soviets, as we try to assess their overall foreign policy intentions, Soviet air forces have traditionally, at least since World War II, tended to invest in a more defensively inclined airplane, the Interceptor, with a shorter range and a lower carrying capacity, but with faster climbing speed. Whenever the Soviet-supplied air forces of Egypt or Syria clashed with the U.S.-supplied air force of Israel, the latter was always better at carrying the battle into its opponent's airspace.)

It may be an accident of production, and nothing to do with intentions, that Soviet ground forces are so well prepared for the offensive, while Soviet tactical air forces are disposed in the opposite direction. Yet, whatever the Soviet intention, the result still gives Moscow capabilities that are worrisome to Western security.

Turning to Western motives again, why have U.S. nuclear weapons been deployed to West Germany and to other locations in Western Europe? Here again we must sort out alternative theories, and perhaps cast doubt on the official pronouncements on such topics.

Officially these weapons are there to defend territory by blunting some future Soviet conventional armored attack. If such weapons do favor the defense, and in this case the numerically smaller side, and if they do not destroy all that is being defended,

then we would have applied nuclear technology in a straightforward manner to solve our problems.[26]

In actuality, however, there is reason to doubt all of these
premises. Theater nuclear weapons may not favor the defense by
knocking out the tank, and they may not favor the side with the
smaller force totals. Above all, the use of nuclear weapons may
damage the territory being fought over.

A second, and very different, explanation for the deployment
of nuclear weapons in Western Europe, in the very path of any
Soviet ground advance, would dismiss all prospects of keeping
such a nuclear escalation limited. Instead, this scenario would
hope that the mere prospect of such a nuclear escalation, by which
Moscow and Kiev and all the other cities of the Soviet Union (and
of the United States as well) would be destroyed, would keep
the Soviets from ever launching such a conventional attack. This
makes the theater nuclear weapons that have been deployed in
one form or another in West Germany since the mid 1950s a trip-
wire, not a substitute, for escalation and deterrence.[27] It desig-
nates the ultimate targets of such weapons as the most valued
real estate of the Soviet Union, while shifting the deterrence focus
away from Moscow's ability to move tank forces forward. This
theory of the role of theater nuclear weapons almost welcomes
the damage that they will do to civilian surroundings, for even
the destruction of West Germany is something of a deterrent to
a Soviet attack.

Here we are entering into the very large topics of "extended
nuclear deterrence" and "nuclear umbrellas," amid decades of
discussions as to what makes such deterrence credible or incredible. Some would argue that only a U.S. "strategic superiority"
in nuclear weapons can make such escalation, with its consequent
extension of nuclear deterrence, believable. Others have contended that only a U.S. nuclear monopoly would make such esca-

[26]As an example of an argument stressing the battlefield defensive uses of tactical
nuclear weapons, see Henry A. Kissinger, *Nuclear Weapons and Foreign Policy* (New York:
Harper and Brothers, 1957), especially chap. 6.

[27]For an argument stressing instead the escalatory coupling properties of a forward
deployment of theater nuclear weapons, see Henry A. Kissinger, *The Troubled Partnership*
(New York: McGraw-Hill, 1965).

lation credible, for what good does a superiority do if the Soviets can still destroy fifty or one hundred U.S. cities?

A straightforward and simple-minded theory will instead be put forward here. Neither a U.S. monopoly nor U.S. superiority (whatever "superiority" can mean) is required in strategic nuclear weapons to keep the escalation threat credible enough to deter Moscow from ever trying to exploit its advantages in conventional weaponry. Rather, what is required is that the United States keeps some of its nuclear weapons physically in the path of any Soviet advance, so that the officers handling those weapons are in a position of "use them or lose them" if the Soviet aggression is making military progress. Gorbachev could be briefed as completely as possible on the details of the permissive action links (PAL) by which such weapons are presumably capable of being locked up and withheld from use by the veto of the president of the United States, but the Soviet leader would still have to worry that some of them might be used (with devastating results for the cities of the Soviet Union).

There is yet a third kind of explanation for the deployment of U.S. nuclear weapons to Europe. This explanation is much less directly related to the threat of Soviet conventional aggression, but it requires that the nuclear systems based in Europe be able to hit targets in the Soviet Union.[28] Such deployments have at times simply amounted to a reassurance as to basic deterrence capability for the United States itself, reinforcing the ability of the U.S. Air Force to strike at Soviet cities in retaliation after the Soviet Air Force had carried out any kind of sneak attack. Back in the days when the bombers of neither side had intercontinental-range capabilities, and when missiles had not yet been perfected, the United States had to base its nuclear weapons at least as far forward as Britain if it was to have an ability to strike at Moscow or Kiev. In the time of the "missile gap" fears, when it looked like the Soviet Union would have ICBMs before the United States perfected any of its own, one U.S. remedy was to deploy Thor and Jupiter intermediate-range missiles forward, to Britain

---

[28]Forward deployments as a reinsurance for basic deterrence are discussed in Glenn Snyder, *Deterrence and Defense* (Princeton: Princeton University Press, 1961), chap. 3.

and Italy and Turkey, in order to assure that U.S. nuclear retaliation would always be able to get through. This was a deployment of U.S. nuclear weapons to locations in Western Europe for more narrowly U.S. purposes: to assure that the Soviets could never launch a nuclear attack on the cities of North America and hope to escape retaliation.

This third kind of motivations for U.S. nuclear deployments in Europe has only applied in the short periods when the retaliatory instruments based in the United States might have seemed threatened. Such forward deployments were a guard against the missile gap, and would have been an additional complication for any "window of vulnerability" (if there had not already been enough other complications to make any Soviet advantages here unreal). For most periods of time, the official explanation of such a deployment would have been the first listed above—its alleged contribution to defense—while the real explanation might have more closely resembled the second—its reinforcement of deterrence, if by nothing more than what Thomas Schelling terms "the threat that leaves something to chance."[29]

There are two important points about any comparison of these motives: (1) how easily the same deployment can serve any one of them, and (2) how the logic of one can blur into the logic of another.

One can illustrate some of this uncertainty about what we have been trying to do with nuclear weapons in NATO by a comparison with something interestingly analogous, but at least as unknowable: what Khrushchev had intended to do with his 1962 deployment of intermediate-range nuclear missiles to Cuba.

Just like the European members of NATO, Cuba is geopolitically vulnerable to the opposing side. Just like NATO, Cuba is valuable for one reason or another (perhaps merely out of a commitment to ideology and principle) to its superpower patron. Just like NATO, Cuba experienced a forward deployment of its patron's nuclear weapons systems.[30]

[29]Thomas C. Schelling, *The Strategy of Conflict* (Cambridge, Mass.: Harvard University Press, 1960), chap. 8.

[30]On the possible explanations for the Soviet deployment of nuclear weapons to Cuba, see Arnold Horelick and Myron Rush, *Strategic Power and Soviet Foreign Policy* (Chicago: University of Chicago Press, 1965).

We can probably rule out any theory that says the missiles deployed to Cuba were somehow intended to repulse another U.S. invasion of the Cuban coast like the one at the Bay of Pigs. There is no explanation as to how nuclear warheads would make the crucial tactical difference here, and certainly not the warheads on the front of such relatively short-range missiles. But the other two theories are both equally credible and compete usefully with each other.

Perhaps the Soviet missiles were placed in Cuba in order to be trip-wire confirmers of escalation, so as to produce an extended nuclear deterrence on behalf of Cuba in case the United States ever felt like putting its full resources into a conventional liberation of the island. (A conventional military invasion is certainly something many Americans might have wished for, to complete our analogy, while almost every one of these Americans would have opposed any nuclear devastation of Cuba.)

Or, instead of an extension of the Soviet nuclear umbrella to protect Cuba, was the deployment intended rather to reinforce Moscow's basic deterrence posture (the Soviet ability to hit targets inside the United States)? As noted earlier, the Soviets had not succeeded in producing ICBMs "like sausages," but they had produced a great number of SS-4s and SS-5s. Just as five years earlier in the case of the U.S. Thor and Jupiter missiles, the movement of medium-range ballistic missiles (MRBMs) forward, when one is short of ICBMs, can make MRBMs the functional equivalent of ICBMs.

Thinking about analogies can sometimes be instructive. To round out the comparison, a few of the Americans speculating about "horizontal escalation" in the 1980s have treated the U.S. geopolitical and conventional military advantage around Cuba as a counter to Soviet aggressions in Europe.[31] This theory says the U.S. grip on Cuba has had the same effect as did the Soviet conventional grip on Europe between 1945 and 1949 (the prospect of an occupation being held in reserve to deter some kind of opposing superpower behavior).

---

[31]The concept of horizontal escalation is outlined in Samuel Huntington, ed., *The Strategic Imperative* (Cambridge, Mass.: Ballinger, 1982).

A skeptic might question whether Cuba can ever be as valuable to the Soviets as Western Europe has been to Americans. Could anyone think of Cuba as "the sixteenth Soviet Socialist Republic"? Yet Cuba has been fairly important to both of the superpowers. When else have Moscow and Washington come as close to an all-out nuclear war as during the 1962 Cuban missile crisis?

Some important themes still need to be noted. First, the United States is not the only member of NATO with nuclear weapons capable of independently devastating Soviet cities. Britain and France acquired such bombs in 1952 and in 1960, respectively. The French nuclear stockpile is the most important, if only for ending speculations about a Soviet thrust to the Bay of Biscay. Even if the United States were someday to cease to be committed to nuclear escalation in defense of its European allies, the farthest the Soviet tanks could roll before incurring nuclear escalation would presumably be . . . Luxembourg.

The French arguments, enunciated for more than two decades now, have been that a nation would never expose itself to nuclear devastation on behalf of a friend, but that it would certainly accept such devastation, and inflict such devastation on the foreign aggressor, if it were itself about to be defeated and occupied in a conventional attack.

At the very least, we will now continually have to consider the implications of this kind of argument for the West Germans. Will they not read the translation of Pierre Gallois as suggesting that an independent West German nuclear force is the solution to all of our problems, the ultimate deterrent to the Soviet threat? Will they feel forever inhibited from taking this step by memories of German behavior during World War II?

One should not count too much on such memories. As each decade goes by, a smaller and smaller fraction of West Germans will feel any personal guilt for the Nazi period. If the Soviet Union were not to ease the inherent threats that we have been discussing, and if the United States were to seem increasingly averse to extending nuclear deterrence, and if the French were to continue to congratulate themselves for having invested in the nuclear *Force de Frappe*, then some West Germans may start to rethink their commitment to forgoing nuclear proliferation.[32]

We must say something also about two continuing themes that are related to our discussions of Soviet threats, "Finlandisation" and "containment." Each is intertwined with discussions and perceptions of the Soviet threat to Europe, but each is difficult to define and test.

"Finlandisation" could be taken to mean a subtle bending of West European choices in the direction of Soviet wishes, simply as the result of the latent threat of Soviet military action. The analogy emerges from the ways in which the Finns have sometimes been careful not to offend the Soviet Union (for example, in their votes in the United Nations) because the Soviets might one day invoke provisions of the Finnish Peace Treaty as an excuse to send their tanks rolling again toward Helsinki.

Finland is a very nice place to live, a place with a great deal of freedom. One's fondest dream is that Eastern Europe could one day be "Finlandised," for this would be a tremendous accomplishment, a restoration of economic prosperity and of personal and political freedom at the price of only a modest reining in of the choices allowed to the smaller neighbors of the Soviets in foreign and defense policies.

Yet, for Luxembourg or Denmark or Italy to have to be as careful as Finland in dialogues with the Soviets would be something of a loss, so that it makes good sense to oppose the Finlandisation of Western Europe. The more difficult task is to determine whether any of this is already happening due to the supposed inadequacies of the U.S. nuclear potential for canceling out the Soviet conventional military threat.[33]

Sorting things out is not so easy here. When West Europeans deny that Finlandisation is occurring, Americans of a more hawkish persuasion sometimes worry that this may be a repression of

[32]For an American journal article actually advocating a separate nuclear force for West Germany, see David Garnham, "Extending Deterrence With German Nuclear Weapons," *International Security* 10 (Summer 1985): 96–110.

[33]The varieties and ambiguities of the notion of Finlandisation are noted in Max Jakkobson, "Substance and Appearance: Finland," *Foreign Affairs* 58 (Summer 1980): 1034–44; and William Pfaff, "Finlandisation," *The New Yorker* 56 (1 September 1980): 30–34.

unpleasant reality, and that the very denial of Finlandisation constitutes evidence of this. We could thus sink here into a major exercise in epistemology, analogous to the debates about whether the United States psychologically dominates its Third World trading partners in the exchanges of "dependencia." The same holds true for trading relationships between East and West, of course. Who gets more power and leverage in the installation of the natural gas pipeline from the Soviet Union to West Germany, the Soviets who supply heat to the Germans or the Germans who supply much-needed hard currency to the Russians?[34]

All relationships based on political, economic, and military power are complicated and subtle. We would naturally like to tie Gorbachev and the Soviet Union into a benign economic web that offers prosperity to his people, while assuring our own people of safety from their potential for military aggression. At the same time, we do not want our own people tied into any web whereby, out of fear of Soviet tanks or missiles, they must pretend to agree with Gorbachev when they do not.

George Kennan enunciated the theme of "containment" in the years immediately after World War II. Its purpose was to clarify for the United States and others just what the United States was now undertaking in the face of a hostile Soviet Union. The containment doctrine basically envisaged a U.S. commitment to manning—economically, politically, and militarily—the barriers against further Soviet expansion. It was hoped that this policy would, in a decade or two, shake Soviet ideological confidence, producing a mellowing of the system within the Soviet Union itself.[35] Several analytical points can be offered about this benchmark of containment. Compared to the noninvolvement and isolation of the earlier American foreign policy patter, this was something much more ambitious. Compared to our occupation and democratization of Germany and Japan, however, this containment policy, as noted earlier, could be seen as something remarkably less ambitious.

---

[34]For the contrasting interpretations of the impact of the natural gas pipeline, see Bruce Jentleson, *Pipeline Politics* (Ithaca: Cornell University Press, 1986).

[35]The fuller ramifications of the notion of containment are discussed in Terry Deibel and John Gaddis, eds., *Containing the Soviet Union* (New York: Pergamon-Brassey's, 1987).

Has containment succeeded? And where? It has succeeded in shielding Western Europe, for no additional territory has fallen under Communist control there since the 1940s. And that is what this chapter has all been about. It has not succeeded elsewhere, however, as a number of Asian, African, and Latin American territories have fallen under Communist rule during that same period, and have come under regimes that are sometimes as slavishly loyal to Moscow as that of Bulgaria.

But has the obverse of containment worked the way Kennan thought that it would in the Soviet Union or in Eastern Europe? If an inability to expand territorially was supposed to shake the Kremlin leadership's confidence, then this did not seem to come about as quickly as Kennan had expected. And it did not seem to work well at all while the containment barrier was still in red on the global map. Perhaps Gorbachev's current questioning of Marxist orthodoxy could be seen as a belated confirmation of the workings of containment and a shaking of Soviet ideological confidence. But this questioning has come only after the 1960s and 1970s succeeded in coloring in the map nicely with big red blotches for Ethiopia, Angola, and Mozambique.

In any event, what has really shaken Gorbachev's self-confidence is not the lack of territorial expansion, but the lack of economic expansion. What is bedeviling Moscow is not so much the failure to win over the working class of West Germany or of France, but rather its rejection by the working class of Poland and by that of Eastern Europe in general.

In short, it has been important for the United States and its NATO allies to "contain" the Soviets. Containment has preserved valuable aspects of political, economic, and social life in Western Europe. But it is not easy to tell whether this preserving of Western Europe has been important in unsettling the Soviet Communist rulers or in otherwise improving the quality of life in Eastern Europe or the Soviet Union.

Why has the United States gone through all of these efforts at containment and at checking the various manifestations of the Soviet threat? Or, to put it another way, why has the United

States committed itself to being possibly perceived as a threat to the Soviet Union?

Some analysts of international relations see all powers as acting in basically the same way—pursuing their own power and well-being. By this kind of "power politics" or "realist" interpretation, the United States would be an "ordinary country." After World War II, the United States needed the industrial potential, manpower, and raw materials of Western Europe both for its upcoming struggle with the Soviet Union and for its own prosperity; hence it was concerned to shield Western Europe from any takeover by Stalin.[36]

A somewhat different explanation is put forward by Marxist analysts of international relations, whether they are presenting the official catechism in the universities of the Soviet bloc or merely presenting what many less restricted academics in Latin America or in Western Europe now regard as self-evident. (Indeed, many U.S. faculty and students also found this explanation persuasive during the Vietnam War.) This view sees the United States as the most capitalist and, hence, the most troublesome country in the world, since capitalism drives a nation to intervention and to gunboat diplomacy in its pursuit of foreign markets for its gluts of overproduction.[37]

This interpretation would have the United States initiating the Marshall Plan and deploying nuclear weapons simply because of its needs for markets. But this Marxist analysis hardly fits the facts. The Marshall Plan certainly led to some goods for which the United States had no need or markets being shipped to Europe, but it also involved the shipment of goods that were scarce in North America. If the motivation behind the U.S. support of NATO has continued to be the pursuit of markets for Detroit and other U.S. capitalist production centers, then why is the balance of trade going so badly for the United States?

One explanation for the continued U.S. commitment to Europe

[36]For an analysis of the United States pursuing power like any other country, see Richard Rosecrance, ed., *America as an Ordinary Country* (Ithaca: Cornell University Press, 1976).

[37]An example of an interpretation that sees the United States driven by the demands of capitalism can be found in Michael Parenti, *The Anti-Communist Impulse* (New York: Random House, 1969).

is a form of the power politics argument: namely, that any experience of having once defended a place sets up issues of precedent thereafter. For the United States to have defended Korea, or West Berlin, or all of Western Europe, and then to have ceased to defend such places, would naturally raise questions in an opponent's mind as to whether the United States was gradually losing its resolve. West Berlin, once defended, must by this theory always be defended, or else the Soviets would be emboldened to challenge U.S. interests around the globe.

Yet the real explanation for U.S. commitments to Europe goes deeper than considerations of power or of markets. It is plausibly intertwined with theories that assert that, since 1945, the United States has been motivated by generous sentiments toward Europe. Most Americans feel ties of kinship to Europe, for this is where some of their ancestors, and most of their dominant political values, have come from. Beyond this, it is from Europe that we got the Magna Carta and all of our philosophical attitudes on life and liberty, and on processes of government and social organization. Americans may identify with the entire world, but they identify particularly much with countries governed by consent of the governed, and the Western European members of NATO have been the most visible and successful examples of such a system.[38]

Americans are ready to escalate to nuclear war in defense of Hamburg (even though this would destroy Hamburg) because they are convinced that Hamburg and Luxembourg are currently much better governed than Dresden or Warsaw—by the standard of consent by the governed, by the standard of an achievement of happiness for anyone living in these cities. One could label such an assumption ideological (even if most Americans pretend not to have an ideology): the assumption is what the Marxists would call "bourgeois liberal" and what Westerners would simply call "democratic." If the Soviets did not believe the opposite, that is, that Dresden is a happier place than Hamburg, we might have much less of a threat to NATO; if Americans did not believe

[38]For a good example of an interpretation seeing the United States as guided by benign and generous motives, see Philip Quigg, *America, the Dutiful* (New York: Simon and Schuster, 1971).

that Hamburg is the happier place, there would not be an American commitment to NATO.

One can also ponder whether the U.S. commitment to political democracy across Europe is even more ideological and principled than the commitment of many Europeans themselves. Frenchmen care about political freedom in France (except for those who would have followed Thorez in regarding the Soviet Army as the embodiment of a different kind of freedom), and Belgians care about political freedom in Belgium. But do the French and the Belgians care so very much at present about freedom in Poland or in Hungary? Do they care at least as much as do Americans? Are Americans better "Europeans" than the Europeans, because of the mixed origins of the American "melting pot" and the philosophical and ideological detachment that comes from being an ocean away? Americans have long believed that the disputes between Frenchmen and Germans, or between Poles and Lithuanians, had to be trivial compared to the dispute between those who favor a free press and those who oppose it. If part of the active U.S. involvement in Europe shows itself in fanning support for the possible liberation of Eastern Europe, then the Soviets will continue to have something to fear.

Is the future of U.S. politics and commitments less predictable and assured than that of the Soviet Union? Despite the continual flow of "agonizing reappraisals" of U.S. commitments, one could argue that the future of Soviet attitudes is more uncertain because of the Soviet need to consider Eastern European attitudes.

U.S. commitments to Western Europe, and to all of Europe, will persist, despite the arguments and the backbiting that go on across the Atlantic.[39] What looks like the collapse of the Western alliance is usually the normal workings of free discussion among free partners in any such alliance. The first "NATO in disarray" editorial appeared in the *Washington Post* in 1951. The U.S. humorist Art Buchwald once offered a fascinating alleged opinion poll. He found that "more Frenchmen hate other Frenchmen than

---

[39]As an illustration of the ways in which NATO has been thought to be in disarray, see Stanley Kober, "Can NATO Survive?" *International Affairs* 59 (Summer 1983): 339–48.

hate Americans." Such disputes are very much "all in the family," and the reality of that family, sharing fundamental values, remains in place. Can the Soviet leadership depend upon a similar resonance by the Eastern European masses with Soviet values? Can it even depend on the support of its own masses within the Soviet Union?

The greatest uncertainties over the future of the U.S. and NATO responses to the Soviet threat concern the nature of that threat, considering all that Gorbachev is now setting into motion. Will the Soviets continue to change their style? Will they change more than style? Will they amend their ideology by dismissing the invitations of Thorez and his like? Will Gorbachev and his partners move ahead with their concessions as to asymmetries in the conventional force balance and finally begin reducing the threateningly large numbers of Soviet tanks? Will they substantially change their modus vivendi with the West?

If Eastern Europe is perhaps the centerpiece and the catalyst for all of these changes (for what better proof is there that the Red Army has no gift to bring to the working class of Belgium than the attitudes of the working class in Poland?), then there is much room for improvement here, and much that could go wrong.

At best, one could have a very benign version of Finlandisation. Moscow could continue to station troops on the territories of its neighbors, retaining a veto over their foreign and defense policies, while allowing all of the current members of the Warsaw Pact to control their domestic situations. This could bring about political freedom and economic prosperity for Eastern Europe. (One rarely hears U.S. or Western European radicals arguing in the case of Eastern Europe, as they often did in the case Vietnam, that the sacrifice of political freedoms was justified by economic gains.)

Yet there are many things that could go wrong. Economic life might not improve so rapidly. Consider all the years in which the Marxist states in Eastern Europe have stamped out capitalist entrepreneurial habits. One could see a reversion to fascism or to antisemitism or to the fierce nationalisms that blame all problems on ethnically different neighbors. After all, these were all typical phenomena in Eastern Europe prior to World War II and the postwar Communist takeovers. One could also see a move to break out of the bonds of Finlandisation, with visibly anti-Soviet foreign and military policies, as Moscow suddenly saw its worst fears of 1945 confirmed.

If even a small part of these possibilities, good or bad, comes to pass, Moscow may well choose to crack down. The results would be a continuation of East-West tension, and a major setback for Gorbachev and his innovations. But it would at least leave Moscow more visibly on the defensive, trying to hold on to the status quo, and the West and freedom seemingly on the offensive.

What military impacts might we expect to come out of this? We might see a reversal of present strategic postures, in which the West employs a no-first-use agreement on nuclear weapons and urges denuclearization, while Moscow talks of "flexible response" and of escalation and allegedly prepares for limited nuclear wars.

Even today, some of our worries about the Soviet threat to Western Europe are eased by these uncertainties about Eastern Europe. Who would want to be a commander of a Soviet armored division going into battle against NATO forces if he had an "allied" Polish division on one flank and an "allied" Hungarian division on the other?

We close on a pessimistic note, however, for we can never be clear as to how any conventional war would be played out in Europe. The loyalties of East European forces are uncertain. But so are the readiness and effectiveness of some NATO armies. The sociological readiness for combat of East and West German soldiers, and of all the other soldiers involved, will also be difficult to predict, not to mention the effectiveness of all the modern weapons being deployed for conventional war. If someone designs the perfect antitank weapon, how many years, or months, will it take until the opponent neutralizes that weapon?

We have a paradox here. We have had no experience with a nuclear war, and yet we may well be able to predict how it could go: It would be a disaster for the world, destroying most of what we were fighting for. On the other hand, we have had many conventional wars since World War II, but we are still typically unable to predict who will win the next one. Each round of fighting in the Middle East offers different lessons on the role of the tank, the role of the fighter-bomber.

In the face of the Soviet threat, Europeans and their U.S. friends long for some certainties. To date, the greatest certainty has stemmed from the threat of nuclear escalation. Unless the Soviets substantially reduce their conventional military threat to the West European peninsula, there is little that Western defensive military preparations alone can accomplish to protect the peace. Despite the revulsion caused by nuclear escalation scenarios, Western Europe and its NATO partner, the United States, may well need to continue to rely on such threats.

14

Doing Business with the Soviets: Sources of Policy Divergence Within the Atlantic Alliance

When President Reagan declared in 1983 that there was "peace among [the allies] on East-West trade,"[1] he was implying that the core differences between the U.S. and European approaches to economic relations with the Soviet bloc, which had sparked such highly divisive controversies in the early 1980s, had been resolved. This prognosis was overly optimistic, and it was based on a limited conception of the nature of these differences. It assumed that they were simply the result of imperfect policy coordination, and thus it obscured the extent to which postwar differences on East-West trade have been more systematic and

---

[1] Robert Putnam and Nicholas Bayne, *Hanging Together: The Seven-Power Summits* (Cambridge, Mass.: Harvard University Press, 1984), p. 181.

134

enduring, prompted by divergent interests, priorities, and phi-
losophies as to both East-West relations and the proper role of
economic tools in foreign policy.

In fact, from the launching of the first complete U.S. strategic
embargo on the Soviet Union in 1949, to the debate over West
European participation in the trans-Siberian natural gas pipeline
in 1982, the formulation of Atlantic Alliance policy on economic
relations with the Soviet Union has been marked by recurring
and, at times, bitter internecine conflict. Throughout the postwar
period, U.S. and European policymakers have debated vigorously the proper use of sanctions and of export controls, as well
as the provision of credit and loans to Eastern Europe and the
Soviet Union. They have clashed just as repeatedly over the long-
term strategic, political, and economic merits of increased trade
with the East. The extent of divergence between the two groups
has varied, but never has it vanished completely. What ideally
should have served as a unifying force in U.S.-European relations—the issue of dealing with the Soviets—has more often
proved to be just the opposite in the realm of East-West economic
policy: a focal point for transatlantic disharmony and a chronic
source of tension among policymakers in allied nations.

There have been many studies of the problem of alliance dis-
unity on East-West trade. But, as this paper will argue, none of
the leading explanations can adequately account for the full complexity and variation over time of the U.S. and West European
policy approaches. In large part, this is because the two most
commonly cited theories of divergence—differences in the *economic interest* and the *geopolitical vulnerability* of Western Europe
and the United States—are based on the unit of the nation. As
such, they are fundamentally statist, static, and home-country
oriented. They each assume that foreign economic policy is
founded primarily on relatively concrete and predictable national
interests and needs, and they each devote little attention to the
role of the less tangible and more elastic perceptions, biases, and
assumptions about the adversary held by individual decisionmakers at the subnational level.

This paper attempts to help to fill that gap. It seeks to examine
the ways in which the images of Soviet aims and capabilities held

by leading U.S. and West European policymakers affect their policy preferences on East-West economic relations. It is based heavily on interviews conducted in 1985 with leading Soviet and foreign policy experts in Great Britain, France, West Germany, and the United States. These analysts were asked to describe not only their policy prescriptions for East-West trade, but also their perceptions of the Soviet Union: the extent of the threat it poses; the role of ideology in Soviet foreign policy; the strength of the contemporary Soviet economy and the degree of potential Western leverage over it; and the impact of economic progress or decline on Soviet international behavior. Each interview was then coded for the analysts' responses to these questions, and cross-tabulations were run by computer to analyze patterns of assessment according to the policy preferences, nationality, political leanings, and occupations of each analyst.

The results were instructive. They indicate that the current fractiousness of the Atlantic Alliance on East-West trade may be due largely to sharply differing assumptions about Soviet behavior held by those who most actively shape national policy choices. The extent of these differences, and their implications for future policy coordination, are explored in greater depth below.

The last ten years have seen an intensification of intra-alliance disputes on a wide range of East-West economic issues. During this time, as throughout the postwar period, the U.S. government has shown a markedly greater propensity than its West European allies to resort to short-term sanctions and embargoes as foreign policy tools against the Soviets. In the most divisive cases, European firms or governments have stepped in to fill orders cancelled by U.S. officials or, as in the gas pipeline affair, the American government has imposed extraterritorial sanctions that have directly interfered with the expectations of European manufacturers and traders. Likewise, disputes have arisen over export controls. Both the Carter and Reagan administrations launched campaigns to tighten existing Coordinating Committee (COCOM) controls, to extend that organization's strategic embargo list to include nonmilitary goods deemed useful to Soviet industrial production, and to intensify enforcement efforts. The

Reagan administration has accused several European governments of allowing a "massive hemorrhage" of banned technology to the Soviet Union.

U.S. and European approaches to long-term trade development have been as clearly out of sync as have policies on sanctions and export controls. U.S. officials have proven consistently less encouraging of trade expansion with the East than have the governments of Great Britain, France, and West Germany. At the same time that the late Carter and early Reagan administrations were seeking, by a variety of measures, to discourage U.S. businesses from increasing their economic interaction with the Eastern bloc, West European governments and leaders were acting to strengthen their commercial and financial ties with the Soviet Union.

Behind these obvious policy differences lie more subtle theoretical disparities as to the proper use of economic tools in East-West relations. Influential U.S. policymakers in the last decade have tended to advocate strategies either of *economic denial* or of *economic linkage*. Proponents of the former urge that transactions with the East be reduced to an absolute minimum, and justify this action with arguments about the permanent competition between Communist and non-Communist societies, the weakness and vulnerability of the Soviet economy, and the contemporary relevance of traditional containment doctrine. The latter school proposes that Western trade and credits be used as levers to extract specific political concessions from the Soviet Union, or, at a minimum, to express approval or disapproval of Soviet internal and external behavior.

Neither of these approaches is particularly popular in Western Europe. Out of more than fifty leading British, French, and West German policymakers interviewed in 1985, virtually none appeared to see any benefit in adopting an economic denial approach. As for economic linkage, these experts generally applauded the use of its positive form ("carrots" or inducements), but remained skeptical of the advantages to be gained from its negative incarnation ("sticks" or punishments).

On the other hand, these European policymakers have proven consistently more willing than their American counterparts to espouse policies of *economic rapprochement*. This third approach is based on the belief that the active encouragement of East-West economic interaction may gradually moderate Soviet behavior by giving the Soviet Union a greater stake in cooperative relations and by encouraging the spread of Western ("liberalizing") ideas in the Eastern bloc. Though this theory is today denigrated in Washington as naive and even dangerous, it is still suggested more frequently than not in London, Paris, and Bonn as a responsible method of encouraging Soviet restraint and of bolstering East-West understanding and accord.

What accounts for these fairly systematic differences both in concrete foreign economic policies and in philosophical or theoretical approaches to economic relations with the East? The two most popular explanations for the long-standing divergence both take as their unit of analysis the "national interest"; analysts routinely attribute disagreements within the Atlantic Alliance either to differing *national economic stakes* in trading with the Soviets or to divergent *geographical or geopolitical vantage points* (Western Europe having a "regional" and the United States a "global" approach to the East). The first explanation draws most of its support from U.S. analysts, the second from West European analysts. But at heart the two groups share a common, rather statist assumption: that foreign economic policies in Western Europe and in the U.S. are founded primarily on concrete assessments of the relatively stable needs and interests of the home countries, and that they are influenced only marginally by the more intangible assumptions, biases, and assessments held by individual Soviet decisionmakers.

In brief, the "economic interest" argument postulates that the unique economic power and self-sufficiency of the United States allows it the luxury of concentrating on overriding political and security concerns, while its smaller and more trade-oriented European partners must, of necessity, weigh domestic economic considerations as well in determining their foreign economic policies. Inherent in this explanation is the assumption that the approaches favored by U.S. analysts (economic linkage or denial, both of which include the options of sanctions and trade disruptions) are somehow more politically legitimate than are European preferences (economic rapprochement) because they are less influenced by "distracting" economic motivations. This view has drawn fairly explicit support from many U.S. analysts, including several leading officials of the former Reagan administration, who have accused the Europeans of being "economically dependent" on trade with the East and thus blinded to the political realities of East-West relations. Subscribers to this belief dismiss European political arguments for rapprochement as largely rationalizations for other concerns.

The theory behind the "geopolitics" explanation, in turn, is that the United States, a superpower geographically detached from the Soviet Union, feels both the freedom and the responsibility to focus on the global balance of power between the East and the West. Because U.S. interests are not directly vulnerable to a Soviet response, U.S. policymakers are ostensibly much less cautious in risking an escalation of East-West tension by employing economic pressure in response to global developments. European nations, by contrast, are constrained by their middle-power status and by their geographical proximity to a hostile superpower: their first priority is not global activism but rather European stability. For this reason they strongly oppose the use of economic pressure tactics (denial or negative linkage) against the Soviet Union; such policies might conceivably be useful responses to perceived Soviet adventurism abroad, but they are also likely to result in a disproportionate increase in tension at the center of Europe.

Despite the apparent power of these two national interest explanations, neither satisfactorily accounts for the full range of phenomena that have characterized the U.S.-European split on East-West trade over time. The omnipresent economic interest theory has numerous flaws. First, it exaggerates the degree of European dependence on East-West trade, both in terms of aggregate figures and of individual economic sectors. Second, it fails to explain why a nation like Britain, whose economic stake in trade with the Soviet Union has declined dramatically in the last few decades to a level roughly equivalent today to that of the United States, still remains hostile to denial policies and to the use of U.S.-style sanctions and negative linkage. Third, the economic interest theory confuses effect with cause: the pattern of fluctuations in the economic dependences of Western Europe and of the United States indicates that a nation's economic stake in trade with the Soviet Union is more likely to be the consequence of its politically determined policy than the key determinant. Finally, the economic interest model fails to provide a mechanism for change which can reconcile the record of dramatic policy oscillations in the postwar period with the fact of relatively stable economic interests during that same period.

The geopolitics theory is also neither wholly convincing nor comprehensive. To its credit, it resolves some of the problems posed by the economic interest model. It helps to explain why European nations with relatively minor economic dependences nonetheless strictly oppose sanctions and trade disruption—as well as why the United States has, at times, proven willing to pursue activist policies that run counter to its *own* economic interest, such as President Carter's grain embargo in January 1980. It also provides a powerful explication of the distinction between global and European detente, and of the European hesitancy to risk gains at its "center" for developments on the non-European "periphery."

But the geopolitics argument still cannot account for the dramatic fluctuations in the U.S. stance on East-West trade over the last forty years; the static nature of geopolitical factors would imply that change should be gradual, proceeding at a glacial pace. Nor can it explain the occasional periods of convergence between U.S. and West European policies, such as during the immediate postwar period, or again in the late 1960s and early 1970s. Finally, the geopolitics approach cannot explain the direction of evolution in U.S. trade policy: Why does the U.S. government appear more willing today to employ sanctions and economic leverage than it was in the late 1960s, when the United States enjoyed a much more powerful strategic position vis-à-vis the Soviet Union?

Of course, neither of the two most commonly cited nation-level explanations of U.S.-European divergence can be completely discarded. They are both undeniably influential in conditioning the policymaking process, and in creating a domestic backdrop of the "acceptable" and "unacceptable" against which decisionmakers must work. They set the outer boundaries of policy options. But within these outer boundaries remains substantial room for maneuver. As this paper will demonstrate, it is within these boundaries that changing patterns of perception, of "reigning ideas" among foreign policymaking elites in individual nations, are so influential. It is not that the personal assumptions and biases of key policymakers can override clear and concrete national interests—but they can play a large role in shaping policy where such interests are ambiguous. They can also provide the impetus for policy change short of drastic realignment of national interest. Finally, they can explain a phenomenon not accounted for by national interest theories, which take for granted that policy is formulated with an eye only toward the home nation's needs and opportunities—that is, why so many policymakers often buttress their prescriptions with speculation about conditions in an adversary nation and with claims as to the objectives and capabilities of the Soviet Union.

Extensive interviews with leading foreign policy experts in Great Britain, France, West Germany, and the United States powerfully support the conclusion that immutable national interest considerations are not alone in shaping national strategies on East-West trade. Rather, the "cognitive presumptions" of decisionmakers about the Soviet Union play an important role: A quite comprehensive syndrome exists in which the positions of European and of U.S. analysts on trade policy are closely connected to their intellectual image of the political objectives and economic conditions of the Soviet Union.

This section of the paper examines five categories of these analysts' presumptions about the Soviet Union: (1) their assessments of the extent of the Soviet threat; (2) their interpretations of the role of Communist ideology in Soviet foreign policy; (3) their estimates of the base-line condition of the Soviet economy; (4) their perceptions of the degree of Western leverage over Soviet economic vulnerabilities; and (5) their beliefs about the impact of economic progress or decline on Soviet international behavior. In each category, U.S. decisionmakers proved to have systematically different attitudes from those of their European peers. Moreover, their individual views of Soviet reality were closely linked to their advocacy of denial, linkage, or rapprochement policies.

As a general principle, contemporary U.S. decisionmakers tended to have what Robert Putnam and Nicholas Bayne describe as a "fundamentally different assessment of Soviet policy from that of most Europeans. The Americans had an image of the Soviet Union at once more threatening (militarily) and more vulnerable (economically)" than the image European policymakers had. Likewise, U.S. experts view the Soviet foreign policy posture as conditioned more by the demands of Communist ideology than do European analysts. U.S. experts estimate Soviet dependence on Western goods and markets to be greater than do most Europeans, and they tend to view that dependence as evidence of the potential power of Western leverage strategies. Finally, the two groups hold contrasting interpretations of the effect on Soviet international behavior of economic progress or decline. While key policymakers in Washington have applauded indications of heightened Soviet economic difficulty as "disarming the adversary," their European counterparts have warned that a "hungry bear" is a vicious one, and that economic insecurity in the Soviet Union could encourage greater nationalism, confrontation, and anti-Western hostility. Both in logic and in practice, the beliefs held by U.S. policymakers tend to lead to policies designed to weaken the (more threatening) adversary, while those held by the Europeans tend to lead to efforts aimed at stabilizing Soviet behavior through enhanced prosperity.

One of the most interesting subnational explanations for U.S.-European divergence on economic policy toward the Soviet Union is that policy preferences of analysts seem to reflect fundamentally different assessments of the extent of the Soviet "threat"—that is, the degree to which Soviet foreign policy is aggressive and expansionist, either by ideology or by traditional state interest. While European analysts tended to stress the cautious and increasingly conservative aims of Soviet foreign policy, the U.S. experts interviewed emphasized the continued commitment of the Soviet Union to overseas expansion and the inevitability of

East-West tension growing out of that threat. These U.S. experts were consistently critical of European statements that Soviet economic problems would deflect that nation from an activist foreign policy. In fact, not one of the U.S. analysts interviewed chose to describe Soviet aims as either "defensive" or as "moderately defensive"; roughly 75 percent of them characterized Soviet behavior as either "extremely" or "moderately aggressive." By contrast, only one of the European respondents described Soviet behavior as anything more dangerous than "moderate." On the three-point scale used to measure the responses to Soviet aims (the higher the number, the more hostilely are Soviet aims perceived), statements of the U.S. analysts averaged 2.6; the average for European analysts was 1.6.

That leading U.S. analysts proved systematically more likely than their European counterparts to stress the "expansionist" nature of the Soviet Union helps to explain why the U.S. government has, in the last decade, commonly favored denial or linkage policies over rapprochement. The correlation between policy preference and threat assessment turned out to be extremely strong: U.S. analysts who advocated denial strategies averaged 2.9 on the three-point scale, while those preferring rapprochement averaged only 1.5 (with a full 40 percent of the analysts taking the least threatened view of Soviet behavior). Linkage proponents fell in between, averaging 1.9 and consistently stressing the moderate and flexible nature of Soviet foreign policy. Thus, those who perceived contemporary Soviet aims as inherently aggressive turned out to favor economic policies designed to minimize the Soviet ability to expand by exploiting its economic weaknesses and by denying it needed goods, equipment, and hard currency. By the same token, those who described Soviet aims as fairly cautious tended to advocate policies aimed at rapprochement; they operated on the assumption that expanding economic interchange could reinforce the perceived Soviet trend toward caution, or even toward complacency. Finally, those with an intermediate view of Soviet aims, one that perceived the Soviet leadership as ready to "push at an open door" but not committed fundamentally to either expansion or retrenchment, generally favored linkage policies—short-term inducements or threats designed to reward restraint and to discourage Soviet decisionmakers from aggressive behavior should discrete opportunities arise.

One final observation about contemporary threat assessments indicates the power of cognitive variables in shaping policy choices. The same interviews that documented systematic U.S.-European differences in threat assessment also demonstrated significant variations within Europe itself: Broadly speaking, West German analysts tended to adopt the most benign views of Soviet behavior and of the efficacy of rapprochement policies, while French experts were the most skeptical. These statistics show an interesting evolution from the early postwar pattern in which French elite perceptions of Soviet aims generally proved to be much less skeptical than were those of the Germans. Thus, while German perceptions of the Soviet threat have been growing more sanguine in the last two decades, French attitudes have been growing less so. If prevalent ideas about the Soviet threat were merely by-products of changes in external variables, such as Soviet behavior, we would expect intellectual attitudes toward the Soviet Union to have moved in the same direction in France and Germany during the 1970s and 1980s, rather than moving in opposite directions toward a point of potential divergence. That the same concrete stimulus (Soviet "reality") produced two such differing readings (an "increasing threat" as well as "a declining threat") in adjoining nations suggests that the beliefs and cognitive presumptions of analysts can have some autonomous origin and role in international affairs.

If U.S. and West European analysts appeared to differ in their assessments of the Soviet threat, they also varied in their perception of the role of Communist ideology in determining Soviet foreign policy goals and behavior. European analysts proved significantly more likely to express skepticism about the ideological motivation of the Soviet Union ("merely a rationalization," commented one) and to interpret Soviet behavior in terms of power politics. Again coded on a three-point scale (with higher values corresponding to perceptions of greater ideological influence and lower values to the primacy of conventional state interest), U.S.

analysts averaged 2.7 while West Europeans together averaged 1.5. Not one of the U.S. experts was coded at less than 2.0, while only one European was coded as greater than that figure. Though these results seem to have little direct effect on trade policy preferences, they do have interesting implications for the development of differing threat assessments on the two sides of the Atlantic. To the extent that a foreign state is seen as motivated by traditional political, historical, geographic, or economic objectives, it is somehow less threatening. A government that responds to these familiar, "statelike" stimuli will likely prove more flexible and rational than one engaged in ideological crusades and to be a government with which, as British Prime Minister Margaret Thatcher puts it, "we can do business."

If divergence within the Atlantic Alliance on economic policy toward the Soviet Union seems to be based, in part, on contrasting perceptions of Soviet aims and intentions, then the views of policymakers as to Soviet internal capabilities appear equally influential. Consider those policymakers with fairly bleak interpretations of the contemporary Soviet economic position, in that they assume a current or impending "crisis" or even a "historical decline." These have tended to promote policies designed either to hasten that decline, by increasing the stress on the Soviet economy and exploiting its greatest vulnerabilities (the denial approach), or, at a minimum, to capitalize on particular Soviet weaknesses by way of inducements or threats so as to gain concessions on political or diplomatic issues (linkage). By contrast, those analysts who have interpreted Soviet economic strains as less severe and inhibiting have been likely to propose policies of rapprochement and trade expansion. Because the Soviet "bear" was, in their eyes, not only here to stay but also in control of formidable resources, they regarded as the best policy for the West the pursuit of a more peaceful coexistence by curbing the bear's appetite.

As early as 1978, a U.S. congressional study concluded that U.S. and West European policymakers differed substantially in their assessment of the state of the Soviet economy. According to this report, European analysts were consistently critical of the

U.S. intelligence community's bleak forecast of the future of the Soviet economy; they saw U.S. estimates both as an exaggeration of Soviet problems and as an underestimation of the ability of Soviet leadership to solve them over time. They were particularly skeptical of the "crisis" view voiced both by certain U.S. intelligence experts and, in the early 1980s, by prominent members of the Reagan administration, including the president himself.

Interviews conducted in the summer of 1985 indicate that the congressional report's findings have not become obsolete. Almost all academics and officials contacted on both sides of the Atlantic agreed with the generalization that U.S. analysts tend to see Soviet weaknesses as more severe than do their European counterparts. The analysts' personal assessments of the Soviet economy reinforced this impression. U.S. officials in both the Pentagon and the State Department did indeed tend to emphasize Soviet weaknesses: Coded on a five-point scale (with higher values corresponding to more dire predictions about the Soviet economy), U.S. assessments averaged 3.75. More interestingly, they were clustered entirely from 3.0 (moderate but incorrectable problems) to 5.0 (imminent crisis or collapse); not one U.S. analyst argued that the major problems in the Soviet economy were potentially correctable in the foreseeable future. By contrast, more than one-half of the European analysts depicted Soviet economic problems as manageable over time; as a group, they stressed the remaining Soviet resources and warned that it would be a mistake to base Western policy on assumptions of economic decline. On the five-point scale, the European analysts averaged 2.7, with over 50 percent of them being coded at 2.5 or below.

If European and U.S. experts differed systematically in their views of Soviet economic strength, they differed even more dramatically in their assessments of the extent of Soviet dependence on Western trade, and thus of the degree of potential leverage Western governments could bring to bear on them. U.S. experts proved consistently more likely than their European counterparts to emphasize Soviet vulnerability to leverage strategies in the form of either linkage or of denial. On a four-point scale (with higher ratings corresponding to assessments of greater Soviet dependence), U.S. analysts averaged 3.4, with fully 36 percent of them taking the extreme position that Soviet vulnerabilities could be exploited powerfully enough to pressure Soviet leadership into significant modifications of foreign policy behavior. The mean rating of European analysts, by contrast, was 1.7—only one-half as large as the U.S. average. Only one out of twenty-seven European respondents admitted to believing that Soviet policy could be influenced at all by Western economic leverage. Instead, the European respondents emphasized the Soviet Union's long autarchic tradition, and they pointed out that the Soviet people were instinctively conditioned to tightening their belts in times of economic stress and to resisting pressure for concessions.

While the analysts' assessments as to the degree of Western leverage were more closely related to their policy preferences than were their beliefs about the base-line condition of the Soviet economy, a third cognitive dimension seems still more influential: their assumptions as to the effect of changing economic fortunes on Soviet international behavior. Would a weakened or a strengthened Soviet economy be more beneficial for Western interests? Do policymakers hope through their actions to increase the instability or vulnerability of the Soviet economy, or to strengthen it in order to stabilize East-West relations? The analysts' positions on this debate are inextricably linked to their interpretation of the so-called "fat Russian/thin Russian" paradox, which questions whether an adversary is more easily handled when domestically prosperous ("content") or domestically weak ("disarmed"). Those who believe that a "fatter" Soviet Union is "distracted from belligerence and hostility," in Paul Hollander's words, and, correspondingly, that a "thinner" Soviet Union is "more nationalistic and militaristic," in Lord Peter Carrington's words, are more likely to favor increasing trade and mutual gain— whatever their view of the Soviet base-line economic condition. Similarly, those who see a fatter Soviet Union as inherently more competitive and a thinner Soviet Union as necessarily less threatening tend to promote policies designed to deny the Soviets goods that would help them compensate for their domestic weaknesses—in essence, limiting trade relations regardless of whether they believe the Soviet economy is on the verge of collapse.

Recent interviews document that the analysts' positions on this "fat Russian/thin Russian" question do in fact influence their policy preferences. Coded on a three-point scale (with higher values indicating hope for resolution of Soviet economic problems and lower values representing expressed desires for the exacerbation of these problems), denial advocates averaged 1.25, with roughly 67 percent of them coding at precisely 1.0. Linkage proponents averaged 2.1, with 67 percent of them coding at 2.0, while advocates of rapprochement averaged 2.8, with a full 78 percent of them coding at 3.0. Once again, differences were also reflected along national lines: U.S. officials proved far more willing to contemplate an exacerbation of Soviet economic weaknesses, while European officials expressed greater hope that the Soviets would achieve security by learning to manage their economic problems. The majority of European experts contended that helping the Soviet Union to maintain economic growth without expansion could calm Soviet insecurity and aggressive tendencies.

The previous pages have shown that the perceptions of analysts as to the nature of the Soviet Union are at least as important in shaping East-West economic policy, and in explaining systematic U.S.-European divergence, as are the more commonly cited factors of "economic interest" and "geopolitical vulnerability." What are the implications of this conclusion for U.S. policy and for alliance unity? That "ideas" appear to play an important policy-shaping role that is independent of interests should be encouraging for those who hope to resolve long-standing intra-alliance disagreement on economic relations with the Soviet Union. National interests, whether economic or geopolitical, are virtually immutable; to the extent that they may be responsible for U.S.-European divergence, policymakers have their hands tied. But ideas are more malleable, especially over longer periods. They are also "manipulable," a variable over which policymakers may have a relatively high degree of control. Beliefs can be altered by bringing them into contact with other conflicting or persuasive beliefs, or by changing the physical or intellectual data upon which they are based.

The implications for policymakers are obvious: To the extent that changes in prevailing ideas can bring with them gradual changes in actual policy postures, today's decisionmakers may have some power to reduce intra-alliance conflicts by working to bring the cognitive presumptions of key actors into closer agreement. In practical terms, this means holding more systematic discussions on Soviet motivations and intentions. It means increased transatlantic data sharing as to the strength of the Soviet economy and its vulnerability to potential Western leverage, sector by sector and under a wide range of conditions. It means conducting more analysis of the "fat Russian/thin Russian" question, and trying to achieve some common assessment of, in Henry Kissinger's words, "those factors in the Soviet Union that produce belligerence and those that encourage moderation."[2]

Of course, consultation and persuasion are not panaceas, particularly when the conflict to be resolved is fairly fundamental and nonquantifiable. As Kissinger wrote in 1965, "Consultation is least effective when it is most needed: when there exist basic differences in assessment or of interest. It works best in implementing a consensus rather than creating it."[3] Moreover, as John Odell points out, merely increasing access to the same information may not bring about unanimity. The same data or historical examples are often interpreted in different ways, depending on the "predispositions that policymakers bring with them when they take office"; thus, for example, the period of detente can be viewed as an illustration of both the success and the failure of rapprochement policy. Robert Jervis explains this phenomenon well in his essay on perceptions and misperceptions in international relations when he writes, "Decision makers tend to fit incoming information into their existing theories and images . . . [so that] actors tend to perceive what they expect."[4]

Nevertheless, some degree of mutual enlightenment is likely to occur in the joint analysis suggested above. To the degree that

[2]Henry Kissinger, *The Troubled Partnership* (New York: McGraw-Hill, 1965), p. 266.
[3]Ibid., p. 227.
[4]Robert Jervis, "Hypotheses on Misperception," *World Politics* 20 (April 1968): 455.

any convergence is possible, or even an agreement on what Kissinger has termed a "permissible range of divergence"[5] between U.S. and European presumptions about the Soviet Union, such exchanges are worthwhile—even imperative. The urgency of this recommendation should not be misinterpreted, of course; it is not that the recurring U.S.-European tensions over East-West economic relations are likely ever to be a serious threat to the future of the Atlantic Alliance. The alliance is founded on firm grounds completely apart from the issue of economic relations with the Soviet Union; it is based on an understanding of the shared security, economic, political, and cultural concerns that unite the United States and Western Europe.

Yet the divergence cannot easily be shrugged off. The East-West trade issue will remain a chronic source of tension for the alliance so long as U.S. policy remains in a position of counterpoint to that represented by the West European consensus—and the persistence of highly divisive conflicts carries its own dangers. Internecine conflict on one issue can sow resentment and distrust, which will distract alliance members from pursuing even their shared goals. In East-West relations, prolonged U.S.-European struggle prevents the alliance from presenting a consistent face to the Soviet Union, thereby hampering negotiations with the East and encouraging the Soviets to try to exploit internal dissension in the West for their own advantage ("wedge driving"). Chronic dispute over East-West economic policy brings other costs to the alliance nations. It raises the disquieting possibility of one nation's policy being consistently undermined by another's, and, in the most divisive cases, may even lead to the use of sanctions and other forms of economic leverage among "friends." Any types of disagreements among alliance partners are regrettable, but these types are more severe—for they rest on fairly fundamental differences of approach and outlook, both as to the conduct of East-West relations and the role of economic policy in foreign affairs.

For all of these reasons, efforts to reconcile European and U.S. attitudes, and to coordinate alliance policies on economic rela-

[5]Kissinger, *The Troubled Partnership,* p. 233.

tions with the East, are vital. They are particularly imperative today—for at a time when the intermediate nuclear forces agreement is altering the debate over U.S.-European security cooperation and creating some new tensions within the Atlantic Alliance, Western policymakers must begin to seek new ways of enhancing alliance solidarity in other, in some ways equally crucial, aspects of East-West relations.

15

NATO
and the Infrastructure
of Reassurance

PAUL Y. HAMMOND

The Marshall Plan was the seedbed of much postwar international activity. At the least, it was influential in setting the style of U.S. foreign policy during the years of maximum U.S. power. The plan provided a way for the United States to reconcile its position as a great power with its democratic politics and with the peculiar requirements of its highly polyarchic constitutional system. It pointed attention to economic growth rather than to redistribution, the preoccupation of the 1930s. And it secured and sustained a transatlantic connection that had been asserted only belatedly in two world wars.

As Charles Kindleberger once put it, the Marshall Plan "never came to an end but was swallowed up in defense activity which developed under the North Atlantic Treaty Organization."[1] On

[1]Charles P. Kindleberger, *Power and Money* (New York: Basic Books, 1970), p. 99.

the U.S. side, grant economic credits for the European Recovery Program changed to grant-based credits and to grant military equipment for mutual security—which is to say, for restoring military defensive capabilities in Western Europe. On the European side, the goal of economic recovery remained the highest priority, one that was agreed to and supported by the United States.

Economic cooperation was an integral part of the Marshall Plan from its inception. But it had produced little significant integration of national economies in the European region by the end of 1951. The economic recovery of Western Europe which the European Recovery Program generated was a recovery of national economies. As they revived, national economic interests asserted themselves within the framework of national governments, offsetting in part the regional economic cooperation that the Marshall Plan itself had engendered.

Western European and U.S. leaders had begun to pay attention to security problems even as the European Recovery Program got underway. After the Czech coup in 1948, Western European officials became worried about a threat to their military security from conventional Soviet forces in Eastern Europe and in the Soviet Union; these worries were particularly intense in France and in Italy, where officials perceived that the Soviet military threat might influence domestic politics.

In Washington, too, worries about Soviet power grew. When the Soviet Union detonated its first atom bomb in 1949, the Truman administration became particularly worried that the deterrent effect of the U.S. nuclear arsenal would soon diminish. It began to plan a massive rearmament effort to cope with what it anticipated would be a new threat of conventional war which U.S. nuclear forces could not deter.

With the outbreak of the Korean War in June 1950, the United States launched a broad rearmament program that tripled its defense expenditures. By the end of the European Recovery Program eighteen months later, the U.S. rearmament effort was well under way, and the rearming of Western Europe was carried along with it. This was the period of the founding of NATO.

None of the economic goals of the European Recovery Program dealt with the transatlantic relationship; yet that relationship was unique, and the most important feature of the Marshall Plan. The challenge from the United States, the response from Western Europe, and the subsequent underwriting by the United States proved to be the most successful U.S. effort at intervention anywhere since World War II. It remains today a model instrument of foreign policy, a preferred mode of operation, and an example of how to influence other governments successfully. Most importantly, it was consistent with U.S. values and procedural requirements. Unfortunately its success has never been matched. It was NATO that built upon the transatlantic relationship established through the Marshall Plan.

Harlan Cleveland and Stanley R. Sloan have given strong meaning to the idea that NATO was a bargain struck between Western Europe and the United States and that its history can be understood as the striking and alteration of that bargain over time. By "bargain" is here meant a complex set of understandings reached among several parties. Sloan explains that the main instruments of the original bargain were the Brussels Treaty (1948), involving Belgium, France, Luxembourg, the Netherlands, and Britain; a U.S. Senate declaration named the Vandenberg Resolution (1948) after Arthur Vandernerg, the senior Republican Senator who sponsored it; and the North Atlantic Treaty. David Calleo has spoken of tensions present from the beginning (see Chapter 7). Sloan reminds us in his book *NATO's Future*,[2] as did Dean Acheson in his memoir, *Present at the Creation*,[3] that the major issues that have plagued NATO throughout its history were not only present but clearly identified when the original bargain was struck. These issues were: (1) how to involve German manpower in the defense of Western Europe without re-creating a German military threat; (2) what the United States would do to contribute military forces to NATO and on what terms; (3) how to keep the burden of Western Europe's defense primarily on Western Europe; and (4) whether, or how much, the European members would commit themselves (in Acheson's

[2]Stanley R. Sloan, *NATO's Future* (Washington: National Defense University Press, 1985), pp. 3–18.
[3]Dean Acheson, *Present at the Creation* (New York: W. W. Norton, 1969), pp. 397–99.

words) to ''balanced collective forces rather than balanced national forces.''[4]

The diplomatic process of putting NATO together was carefully choreographed. The Brussels Treaty signatories had been signaled in advance to expect a U.S. response. Senator Vandenberg, the chairman of the Foreign Relations Committee in a Republican-controled Senate, was coached by the State Department to sponsor a resolution that would express Senate support for ''regional and other collective self-defense'' and thus back the Democratic Truman administration in its intent to join with the Brussels powers. Vandenberg's resolution passed the Senate in June 1948. The North Atlantic Treaty was signed in April 1949 and was ratified promptly by the U.S. Senate. ''It was a deal,'' Sloan has written

> struck among governments, to be sure, but with the clear implication that two branches of the American Government were parties to the deal, and that management of the bargain would be a shared responsibility so long as the alliance endured.[5]

Such has been the case, though often to the discomfiture of Europeans. But that discomfiture was—and is—unavoidable. The Truman administration had early on involved the Senate leadership in order to avoid the problem that President Woodrow Wilson encountered with the League of Nations Treaty after World War I. But partnership with Congress was even more essential for putting the treaty into effect. At the time the Senate ratified it, the nature and extent of U.S. involvement in the actual defense of Western Europe remained unresolved, or at least undisclosed. When the prospect arose, as it soon did, of stationing U.S. troops in Europe permanently, the partnership with Congress became unavoidable. The Senate debated the issue following an announcement by Truman that he intended to send a substantial number of troops to Europe, and that the number would depend on ''the degree to which our friends match our

[4]Ibid., p. 398.
[5]Sloan, *NATO's Future*, p. 5.

action.''[6] Much of the Senate's attention was on the legality of the president's action. In this respect, the debate sounded something like what one might hear in the 1980s in either house of Congress with reference to the president's adherence to the War Powers Act. Whether a president could send troops to Europe without the prior consent of the Senate, he certainly could not maintain them there over time without congressional funds. Congress often debates constitutional legalities when it anticipates that, where its constitutional powers are clearer (its control over appropriations), the administration will confront it with embarrassing choices (backing or failing to back an existing military commitment).

The NATO we know today took shape rapidly at the beginning of the 1950s. The key steps included the authorization of an integrated military command, the Supreme Allied Command of Europe (SACEUR), headed by a U.S.-appointed military officer; arrangements for a permanent civilian structure; the admission of Greece and Turkey to membership; and a compromise with the French which permitted German contribution to NATO (but no initial German membership). In 1952, U.S. press accounts stated, according to a State Department cable, that the "entire NATO defense program is facing collapse.''[7] But NATO quickly became part of the landscape of foreign relations for Europe and the United States. More importantly, it became a functioning, routine, everyday part of their national security policies. Yet attention has often been devoted to what NATO fails to do, or does badly, rather than to what it does minimally well. The crises so often reported about NATO have become something of a joke. (NATO is always in a crisis, yet NATO always survives.) One welcomes the occasion for a little humor in international affairs, but this crying wolf conceals the enduring features of the organization. NATO assumed from the start a functional utility for its members, which accounts for much of its resilience.

From the outset, within the constraints imposed by limited con-

---

[6]Quoted in ibid., p. 11.
[7]Quoted in ibid., p. 19.

ventional forces and the uncertainties of reassurance, member governments have used NATO as a solution to some of their stickiest foreign policy problems. David Calleo has touched upon a fundamental problem for Britain and for France: How could they commit military forces to points outside of Europe which were adequate to protect their global security interests? NATO helped them to do so by allowing them to minimize their European military commitments. France wanted to involve the United States in Europe permanently. It found that the United States required, as a condition for its own participation, West German rearmament, which the French had every reason to be alarmed about. NATO gave France the means to commit the United States. After France had attempted to work out a different solution for the West German military contribution through the European Defense Community, NATO also became for France the means for assuring some control over German armed forces.

France, of course, withdrew from NATO in the late sixties. We might suppose that France is hardly the best example to turn to for evidence of the utility of NATO to its members. But the French withdrawal does, in fact, make the point strongly, for France continues to rely on NATO in at least three important respects.

First, France counts on NATO's forward strategy on the central front to deal with a conventional military threat before it reaches the French border. French troops are effectively a NATO reserve force. Recently, as the French government has taken a more cooperative stance toward NATO institutions, this reserve role has become entirely clear.

Second, France has continued to rely on NATO to ensure that the West German armed forces will serve a European purpose. The continuing French anxiety over West Germany has recently been confirmed by French initiatives for bilateral military cooperation with West Germany. These initiatives may denote a declining reliance on NATO. More likely, they supplement and strengthen NATO by drawing France into closer military cooperation.

Third, NATO has satisfied the French interest in assuring a continuing U.S. military presence in Western Europe which includes both conventional and nuclear forces. French diplomacy has recently demonstrated once again the French interest in keeping the United States involved in Western Europe through NATO.

So much for the French case—the case of the nonparticipant. For NATO members who participate in NATO bodies and contribute forces to NATO military commands, the reliance on NATO runs deeper. British ground, naval, and air forces assigned to NATO are routinely justified, within the British government, simply by virtue of that assignment. For the British government, the British Army of the Rhine is a costly commitment that is periodically reviewed and may ultimately be reduced significantly. But such a reduction, should it occur, will not discredit the evidence of decades of relatively stable commitment. For this commitment, the British government gets, in return, assurance of a role in its collective defense. That is a military justification that has been, at least until recently, acceptable to left, center, and right opinion leaders in Britain. Furthermore, British participation in NATO also assures Britain the cooperation of the United States in the provision of nuclear delivery vehicles—including the Polaris, and now the Trident, missile systems. Without these systems, Britain could not make convincing claims to being a nuclear power.

Leave out the factor of independent British nuclear forces, and much the same analysis applies to Italy, Belgium, the Netherlands, Denmark, Norway, Greece, Turkey, and now Spain. These states rely on NATO as a major component of their foreign policy and, with exceptions, as the major rationale for their own armed forces. From a NATO perspective, or at least a U.S. perspective, it is usually the shortfalls in performance that draw attention. Why do not these states (why, indeed, do not all the European members of NATO?) integrate their forces and procurements to achieve economies of scale? Acheson insisted that this question be addressed at the North Atlantic Council Meeting in London in 1950.[8] Critics argue that these governments are free riders. The free-rider argument assumes that they act with the logic of unitary actors. It holds that members will not pay their fair share— in this case, that they will leave it to other states to carry the

[8]Acheson, *Present at the Creation*, p. 398.

burden when their share is not enough to make a significant difference in the total effort.

A sounder charge is that smaller powers, along with larger ones, economize any way they can on their policies and commitments. The smaller powers have reduced to a routine their commitments to NATO. They routinely accept their role in it and its usefulness to them. One measure of the utility and underlying resilience of NATO, if not its success, is that it is taken so much for granted. Even the alarms about NATO are now largely taken for granted.

The free-rider argument is correct in noting how essential it is for NATO members that the United States meet its NATO commitments. Reflecting this fact, European members need "reassurance"—I employ Michael Howard's apt term here—that the United States will keep conventional forces stationed in Europe for deployment in support of the forward strategy and that it will assign nuclear weapons for the same purpose, as well as to deter any attack. This is the easiest part of the reassurance that they need. They also need reassurance that the United States will employ nuclear weapons before a defensive conventional war destroys Western Europe. Some evidence that this reassurance is indeed felt can be gleaned from the fact that the force postures of the smaller powers, as associated with the conventional and nuclear commitments of the United States, are thoroughly routinized. At a critical time in the midsixties, when the United States withdrew its support for a multilateral nuclear force, it brought representatives of NATO member governments into its nuclear-planning apparatus, where they could observe the routines of planning for the employment of U.S. nuclear weapons. By most accounts, this move provided—and still does—some reassurance, although its effect was limited. Those plans, necessarily secret, can reassure only a few Europeans.

West Europeans have reason to be reassured by looking more broadly at the way the U.S. government works. This is true despite the fact that its workings sometimes generate alarm instead of reassurance in Europe. The NATO commitment is built into the routines of U.S. foreign relations. It is a central part of the infrastructure of U.S. foreign policy. Supporting NATO is the largest mission of the U.S. armed forces, which constitute major interest groups in the United States (even their most ardent supporters acknowledge that). NATO thus helps to routinize, and routinely legitimize, U.S. policy.

These functions are part of the tendency in any government to economize on the political costs of its policies. Normally, governmental transaction costs for major, explicit policies in the United States are high. The main elements of U.S. foreign policy have been designed around a series of commitments, which are embodied in annual budgetary transactions. The way these transactions are arranged and carried out minimizes transaction costs, as well as the price that has to be paid for political group consensus.

The strong pluralism of the U.S. government certainly makes it difficult for its commitments to be credible to foreign governments. This difficulty has been partially offset by institutionalizing foreign policy in programs and other tangibles. With respect to Europe, this institutionalism is associated primarily with NATO. The U.S. troop commitment to Europe is a source of reassurance (an attack on Western Europe means an attack on U.S. forces). It is also reassuring because the U.S. commitment to Europe is built into a large, and necessarily ponderous, process of executive and legislative action, of budgeting and authorizing, and of programming military forces years in advance. Most of these actions, even most of these actions that are discretionary, have become routine. They tend to follow observable patterns from one year to the next. To break out of these patterns requires extraordinary efforts. It is in this sense that I use the term infrastructure to refer to U.S. governmental processes that encompass NATO.

Much of the advantage of the NATO infrastructure in Europe and in the United States can be summed up in this way: By reducing their NATO-related activities to routine procedures, and by maintaining a prestigious multilateral authority to tell them their duties, NATO has permitted its members to minimize their dependence on active public support. Public acquiescence, of course, is essential in democratic governments. In the case of NATO, it has been forthcoming—albeit, of late, more erratically.

But NATO has helped member governments to carry on their national security policies without having constantly to work up active public involvement. We speak of consensus in NATO, or more recently, of a loss of consensus. It is not at all clear that the narrow elite consensus on which NATO has long relied has collapsed. What is clear is that NATO, during the early eighties, drew more public attention than is normal, and that opposition groups coalesced and became extremely active for a short time. The surprisingly active opposition that developed in northern Europe in the early eighties over the prospect of deploying Pershing 2 and cruise missiles there, and the speed and the extent with which that opposition diminished, convey two opposing lessons. One is that, since the public is normally quite inattentive and indifferent to NATO, public opinion can be rapidly aroused, given the right conditions. The other is that the result, an aroused public (actually, a minority) highly active in its opposition will not, or may not, long remain so engaged with the issue that aroused it.

This point has broader application. To incumbent politicians, the appeal of NATO as an institution that embodies policy in ordinary governmental and transgovernmental activities is that it permits them to be committed, while reducing their exposure to political attack from opponents outside the government who are not responsible for these commitments. Henry Kissinger provided a striking example of this phenomenon—of the greater maneuverability of the politician out of office—in his oft-quoted statement in Brussels in 1979, on the occasion of the thirtieth anniversary of NATO:

I have sat around the NATO Council table in Brussels and elsewhere and have uttered the magic words which had a profoundly reassuring effect, and which permitted the ministers to return home with a rationale for not increasing defense expenditures. And my successors have uttered the same reassurances. And yet if my analysis is correct, these words cannot be true indefinitely; and if my analysis is correct we must face the fact that it is absurd in the 1980s to base the strategy of the West on the credibility of the threat of mutual suicide.[9]

The candor of this statement is dazzling. Kissinger said what he said he never would say as secretary of state. Why? Because the U.S. secretary of state plays a public role that constrains what he says publicly. More than likely, he would not, while in office, speak ill of arrangements that his government has relied upon as part of its foreign policy infrastructure, however imperfect he may privately regard them. Incumbents do not say such things, for they depend upon existing arrangements.

We usually do not, in the way we analyze and interpret foreign policy, take account of how much we rely on routines, on everyday arrangements, on ordinary practice—on what I have called the infrastructure of foreign policy. So we are at a disadvantage in interpreting that to which we often direct our main attention—exceptional behavior. Europeans have, by now, had long experience coping with the U.S. government, and many of them are very good at it. They often know better than we do how we really behave. Yet I am also struck by how we really behave better than we realize, and how often European observers of the United States view U.S. behavior on a single scale from isolationist to Europeanist. I am surprised to hear remarks describing Senator Sam Nunn as an isolationist, and to hear people attributing isolationism to former senator Mike Mansfield, Nunn's predecessor as a sponsor of resolutions and amendments that threaten to withdraw troops from Europe. Nunn, like Mansfield, has recognized the resilience—and recalcitrance—of the infrastructure that lead them both to rely on NATO while devising measures that could serve as leverage to change it. In both of their cases, I see a highly developed sense of where they sit in the infrastructure and of what is appropriate behavior for them, considering where they sit, and given their abiding commitment to U.S. involvement in Europe (but not necessarily a commitment on the terms that they have developed). In this, I share David Calleo's

[9]Kenneth A. Myers, ed., *NATO: The Next Thirty Years* (Boulder: Westview Press, 1980), p. 7.

sense that the hegemon may be disadvantaged, as well as advantaged, by his hegemonic role (chapter 7).

The issue today is not whether the United States will turn inward the way it did between the two world wars, but whether the country will continue to accord Western Europe the priority that it has previously held in U.S. policymaking. Isolationism drew its original strength from the scale and polyarchy of the governmental process in the United States, as well as from the outlook of voters and their representatives. A major problem over the years, beginning with NATO, has been how to get the United States committed credibly and permanently.

The United States is hard to commit because of its ponderous governmental processes. The Marshall Plan was, in this respect, a brilliant policy innovation in the United States. It turned a mood of rejection of the tools of foreign relations (in effect, a rejection of an international role for the United States) into a constructive engagement of those governmental processes with Europe. The set of commitments that began with the Marshall Plan and went on to include NATO, the mutual assistance programs, and the stationing of sizable forces in Europe engaged Congress with the executive branch in much the same manner as do domestic programs. These instruments of foreign policy generated powerful clienteles in both of these branches of government. Watching the governmental process in Washington, so conspicuously adversarial, one might suppose that the congressional partner in foreign policy contains no supportive clientele groups, only opponents. Opponents of NATO in Congress there are, of course, but the relatively stable pattern of acquiescence there indicates that one can also find supportive clientele groups. The Congress, like the executive branch, has a stake in NATO, just as it retains a stake in presidential initiatives in foreign relations, even while it complains about NATO.

Finally, as international institutions go, NATO has been a major asset for U.S. defense policy. In addition to performing the functions of a multinational military command apparatus, it has performed a variety of underlying and supporting functions. It has justified for Europeans and Americans the presence of U.S. forces in Europe. It has helped West European governments to justify their national military efforts to their own political elites and publics. It has softened the domestic confrontation between right and left in Europe by diminishing the identification of nationalism with military preparedness. It has provided an international framework for the rearmament of West Germany and serves today to reassure all of Europe that the West German Army is under control. It has enhanced the credibility of the U.S. commitment to the defense of Western Europe, although never to the satisfaction of the United States. In the United States, it has enabled successive presidencies, as well as the Congress, to commit themselves to the defense of Europe through routine administrative and annual legislative measures. It once aroused, and still encourages, the hope that Western Europe will unite politically, a remote possibility that would have important strategic implications.

The value of many of these functions has declined. The capacity of NATO to legitimize national military efforts and to distribute military burdens among its members has weakened. It no longer moderates—not, at least, to the degree that it used to—national partisan conflicts over defense policy, because military issues have taken on new ideological forms, such as the Green movement in West Germany or, more broadly, the antinuclear movement. NATO still sometimes softens ideological confrontations between publics and national governments over national security matters. But more recently, it has also supplied the principal issues for such confrontations.

NATO does nothing well enough and nothing badly enough, from the standpoint of its members, to induce them to change it—so far. It survives. To its members, it has become a sunk cost that facilitates the formation and execution of their foreign and defense policies. Profound differences have persisted for nearly four decades among NATO members, and to some extent within member governments, regarding the requirements for deterrence, the role of conventional war in NATO strategy, the criteria for burden sharing, and other important matters of NATO business. These differences are resolved, if at all, only temporarily, usually superficially, and often by symbolic actions and by rhetoric. Resolution by these means leaves real conditions unchanged.

Has NATO in this respect run out of time? Some have taken public agitation over the deployment of intermediate nuclear forces to suggest that it has. But I believe that this agitation does not indicate, as is commonly supposed, that the consensus supporting NATO has been broken. It does suggest, however, that NATO needs a wider base of support in member countries if it is not to be vulnerable to such flare-ups of public attention and opposition. Meanwhile, the prospect of major reductions and other alternations in the force composition of NATO, as well as changing perceptions of the military threat, suggests that the routines of reliance on NATO by its members may have to change. These developments of the early and late 1980s show that we need to understand better than we do now what functions NATO participation performs for the member governments on both sides of the Atlantic.